NERITAN CEKA

ARCHAEOLOGICAL TREASURES FROM ALBANIA

Volume II

Migjeni

MINISTRIA E TURIZMIT, KULTURËS, RINISË DHE SPORTEVE

This album was published on the occasion of the 100th anniversary of the Independence of Albania.

© PUBLISHING HOUSE *Migjeni*
All rights reserved.

Editor: Angjelina Ceka

Translated by: Kathleen Imholz and Pranvera Xhelo

Graphic art by: Sonila Krashi

Front cover: Marble statue of Agrippina Junior, mother of Nero, Buthrotum.
Back cover: Foot of a large bronze vase in the shape of a sphinx, Antigoneia.

ISBN 978-99943-943-7-1

PUBLISHING HOUSE *Migjeni*
Rr. "Ymer Kurti" 2/2/36 Tirana, ALBANIA
Phone: +355 4 2250200
e-mail: migjeni.books@gmail.com
www.migjeni-books.com

CONTENTS

Berat (Partha) 5
Dimale 15
Byllis 17
Amantia 83
Olympe 93
Aulona (Vlora) 97
Kanina 99
Treport 100
Oricum 101
Gramma 107
Palasa (Paleste) 111
Himara and Borsh 115
Onchesmus (Saranda) 130
Phoenice 135
Mesopotam 139
Buthrotum 143
Ancient centres around Buthrotum 195
Antigoneia and the ancient centres around it ... 201
Glossary 231
Origin of illustrations 234

The quarter Mangalem of Berat.

BERAT (PARTHA)

The Castle of today's Berat has in its foundations the walls of an ancient Illyrian city, which has traditionally been identified with Antipatrea. In fact, the position and importance that the Castle of Berat had in antiquity correspond to the Illyrian city Partha, the capital of the *koinon* of the Parthines, who are mentioned by ancient authors as living in the land behind Apollonia and Dyrrhachium. The Parthines are mentioned as allies of Rome from the time of the first Roman-Illyrian war and up to the complete destruction of the Illyrian kingdom in 168 BC. For this reason, they had local autonomy, which they kept until 39 BC when they rebelled against Rome. They were soundly defeated by the army of Consul Asinius Pollio.

Partha is mentioned as a city only two times: in 198 BC, when the Romans surrendered it to the Illyrian king Pleuratus (Polyb., XVIII, 47, 12) and in 48 BC, when it was conquered by Caesar (Bell. Civ., III, 41, 1) during his march from Apollonia to the river Genus (Shkumbin).

The ancient city extended over the upper part of a hill that rises over today's city of Berat, on the right side of the river Osum. Traces "in

View of the Castle of Berat, over the gorges of Osum.

The tower over the main gate of the castle; in the basement: the Illyrian wall of the middle of the 4th century BC.

The North - western tower of the Castle of Berat. 9th century AD.

The main gate of the Castle of Berat. Middle of 4th century BC with different reconstruction in the Middle Ages.

Epheb. Marble stele of Attic production, found in Perhondi, near Berat. End of the 5th century BC.

Farewell to the deceased husband in presence of Hermes. Stone grave stele of local production, found in Lapardha. 3rd century BC.

situ" and blocks reused in the medieval fortifications show that its plan had the form of a triangle with an area of 9,60 ha. The principal entrance is on the north, with a tower over arches placed on top of it, as in Byllis. Also corresponding to Byllis is the isodomic construction technique of walls with quadratic blocks of equal height.

Archaeological excavations have shown that the beginnings of life in the Castle of Berat correspond to a proto-urban period (6th – 5th centuries BC), while the construction of the surrounding walls was realised immediately after that of Byllis, about the middle of the 4th century BC.

The city continued to be inhabited without interruption even during the Roman conquest, while its walls were rebuilt during Late

The church of the Trinity in the Castle of Berat. 14th century.

Altar of Roman period, reused in the same church.

Paleochristian architectonic elements reused in the wall of a church in the Castle of Berat.

The St. Helena Church in the Castle quarter of Berat.

The porch of the Cathedral church in the Castle of Berat.

The St. Michael Church on the rocks of the Castle of Berat.

The city quarter of Gorica and the Illyrian Castle above it.

Street in the quarter Kala, inside the castle of Berat. 18th century.

Summer scene in a street of quarter Kala.

Antiquity (4th – 6th centuries AD). After being abandoned during the early Middle Ages, the castle was rebuilt in the Ninth century, when it was also conquered by the Bulgarians.

Today's name comes from this period, when it was called Bellograd – the white city, perhaps a translation of the old name Partha – Bardha ("white" in Albanian).

Facing the Castle of Berat, on the other side of the Osum on the hill of Gorica, a small ancient castle has been found. It had a surface area of only 0,8 ha and was built in the second half of the 4th century BC to complete the control of the mouth of the Osum.

DIMALE

Dimale was located near the present-day village of Krotina, 20 km from Apollonia. It controlled the road that went from that city to Berat and further through the valley of the Apsus, toward Macedonia.

The city was identified through reading seals on the tiles of the city's workshops, which bore the name of an urban community: ΔΙΜΑΛΛΙΤΑΝ (of the citizens of Dimale). In historical sources, the city is mentioned for the first time in 215 BC as a strategic centre under the control of the Romans who were clashing with Philip V of Macedonia in the lands behind Apollonia (Polyb., VII, 9, 13). In 205 BC, Dimale is mentioned as a neighbour of the Parthines and cities of Bargullum (Margëlliç) and Eugenum (Gurëzeza), always in the context of the conflict between Rome and Macedonia (Liv. XIX, 12, 3). There was also another city by the same name on the Dalmatian coast, facing the island of Pharos (today's Hvar), which played a role during the second Roman-Illyrian war in the years 219-218 BC (Polyb., III, 18, 1).

The hill on which the city stretched out was crowned by a plain with an area of 18 ha, dominated by two low peaks that appear to have given the city its name (the Albanian for two peaks is **dy male** – **Dimale**). Around them, traces can be made out of a wall of rectangular sandstone blocks, which served as a *krepis* for a brick wall, according to the Apollonian model.

The plain between the two peaks was the *agora* of the city, and two *stoas* have been excavated there. The earlier one is found on the southeast side of the *agora* and represents a copy of the Apollonian *stoa* with niches. It has smaller dimensions, only 29,4 m (100 ancient feet), with seven semicircular niches. Its construction belongs to the beginning of the 3rd century BC.

The excavations of 1964 in the ancient stoa of Dimale.

The stoa of Dimale. End of 4th century BC.

Herm of a woman in Illyrian dress, found in Dimale. First half of the 2nd century AD.

Stamp of the koinon of Dimalians in a tile found in the excavations. 3rd century BC.

A second *stoa*, from about half a century later, was excavated in the western side of the *agora*. Its dimensions are 50 x 7,80 m, with two passages separated by wooden colonnades. It served as a market for the city.

Archaeological excavations have shown that urban life began to be developed in Dimale during the second half of the 4th century BC. During the 3rd – 2nd centuries BC, the city was a centre of commerce and production. On the basis of the seals on ceramic products, there were about 17 workshops of this type. During the 2nd – 1st centuries BC, the city went into decline, until it was completely abandoned, perhaps because of the uprising of the Parthines in 39 BC.

BYLLIS

THE HISTORY

With its dominant position over the hills of Mallakastër and a striking view of the breadth of the valley of the Vjosa, the Illyrian settlement of Byllis offers us a perspective completely different from that of the cities of Apollonia and Buthrotum. Byllis was the largest city in Southern Illyria and the capital of the Illyrian community of the Bylliones.

The earliest source for its history is the Greek geographer Pseudo-Scylax, who wrote around 380 BC that "the people of Oricum live in the region of Amantia; the Amantes, who extend up to here, are Bylline Illyrians". In fact, the city plan of Byllis and the techniques of construction of its walls go no earlier than 370-350 BC. Apparently, it was economic growth that led to the decision of Bylline community to build Byllis as their capital in one of the dominating hills over the natural road from Apollonia and coastal Illyria to Epirus and into Macedonia.

The events that transpired in the lands of the Bylliones left no evident traces in Byllis, at least not until the end of the 3rd century BC. A calm and prosperous period characterized the decades up to the appearance of the Romans in Illyria. It was a period distinguished by political co-existence between the Illyrians kings and the cities. By approximately 270 BC, the Bylliones had completely constituted their *koinon*. We can reconstruct its political system from the many inscriptions found in Byllis and Klos. The *prytanis,* who was elected annually according to a custom borrowed from Apollonia, stood at the head of the executive

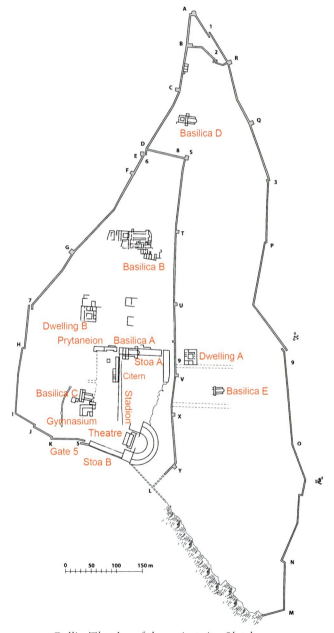

Byllis. The plan of the ancient city. Sketch.

The hill of Gradishta, where the ancient city of Byllis was situated.

Aerial view of Byllis.

power. Several Illyrian names are found among those of the *koinon's* officials, such as Aspimas, Paton, Praugissos, Triteutas, etc.

The *koinon* of the Bylliones also minted its own bronze coins, from around 270 BC until 167 BC, when the Romans dissolved the *koinon*. One type of coin represented the famous fire of the *Nymphaeum*, which, according to Pliny, was found at the border between Apollonia and the barbarian Bylliones and Amantes.

Around the middle of the third century BC Byllis, had the appearance of a contemporary city with the theater, stoa, stadium, gymnasium, temples and other buildings having been constructed. The quarters of the city were developed along a grid or hypodamic system.

Since 229 BC, when the Romans landed in Apollonia, the territory of the Bylliones became a field of battle between the Roman and Macedonian armies, as both Rome and Macedonia appreciated the strategic importance of this region for the control of Apollonia. According to the Roman historian Livy, in 167 BC the Roman consul Paullus Aemilius sent "…his son, Quintus Maximinus, with part of the army, to loot the Illyrians who had supported Perseus in the war and an order was given for them to meet with him in Oricum." Those Illyrians were doubtless the Bylliones, as is shown by traces of terrible destruction in Gurëzeza, Margëlliç and Klos. It is possible that Byllis itself was not destroyed during this campaign and the Romans recognized the status of *koinon* only to that city, which continued to mint its own bronze coins.

The Bylliones appear again in the light of history in the notes of Caesar about the Civil War with Pompey, when are understood to operate as an autonomous unit, taking Caesar's side as soon as he conquered Apollonia.

Byllis was turned into a Roman colony in the first years of the reign of Augustus, as is shown by several Latin inscriptions found there referring to the city as **Colonia Iulia Augusta**, as well as Pliny's characterization of Byllis as a colony. The city walls were rebuilt,

View towards the Vjosa valley from the ancient walls of Byllis.

The Gate of Agora with the inscriptions of Augustus, giving access to the theatre. Reconstructed by the Roman colonists. First half of the 4th century BC.

The Gate of Agora. Ideal reconstruction.

showing the Roman status and power of the city. The theater and stoas were reconstructed, and other monuments were erected. Luxurious residences paved with mosaics showed that there Roman veterans were installed. After an inscription engraved on the rocks of the city, one of them, Marcus Lollianus, paid for the building of a road connecting Byllis with the region of Astacia. Outside of Byllis, in Qesarat, a Roman villa is documented by findings of sculptures, architectural elements and polychromatic mosaics.

Not until the 5th century AD do we meet Byllis again in the ancient sources. In 431 AD, Bishop Felix of Apollonia and Byllis took part

View towards the Vjosa valley from the gate of the agora.

The Northern Gate of Byllis on the road to Apollonia. First half of the 4th century BC.

Part of the surrounding wall of Byllis. First half of the 4th century BC.

*The Round Tower.
End of the 3rd century BC.*

in the council of Ephesus along with the bishops of Dyrrhachion and Scodra representing the Byzantine province of Epirus Nova. By the year 458, Byllis has a bishop of its own (*Philocarus, episcopus Ballidi*). During the reign of Emperor Justinian (527-565 AD), Byllis is mentioned as one of the principal cities of New Epirus. It was Victorinus, one of the rulers of Justinian, who rebuilt the city walls, destroyed by Slavs in 547-551 AD. There are five inscriptions dealing with his works in Byllis. We read in one of them: *"I complain no more about the barbarians, I am no longer afraid, because I found in the Great Victorinus, a man who built me with his hands."* After the last destruction of the city by the Slavs in 586 AD, the seat of the bishopric was moved to Ballsh, preserving the name of the old city, transformed over the centuries from **Byllis** to **Ballis** and finally to **Ballsh**.

THE MONUMENTS OF ILLYRIAN AND ROMAN PERIOD

THE CITY WALLS

The surrounding walls of Byllis are among the best preserved and most majestic works of ancient Illyrian fortifications. They are 2250 m long and enclose an area of 30 hectares over which the ancient city extended.

The walls were 3.50 m thick and were made of limestone blocks worked into rectangular forms and set in almost equal rows. The height of the wall from the outside ranged from 8 to 9 m, while on the inside, there was a pathway for the guards at the height of 3.50 to 5.30 m. Seven gates have so far been discovered, which assured the rapid movement of residents and visitors to the city. The Gate no. 5, leading to the agora from the south, had the look of a real building, with a tower rising over the entrance corridor erected on arches 8.80 m high. This gate was rebuilt when the Roman colony was established. A Latin inscription in a block on the right side of the entrance says *"Augustus, son of the emperor, divine Caesar, permitted it {the rebuilding of the walls}"*.

The city walls of Byllis were built approximately in the second quarter of the fourth century BC. A second period of building took place between 230 and 176 BC, when a round tower with a diameter of 9.60 m was also built. An inscription in ancient Greek, on a stone block of this wall says: "This is dedicated to the gods. When Trasos, son of Hieron was *prytanis* and Melanthos, son of Anthropiskos was *strategos*, (this wall was built) with booty taken from the enemy."

THE AGORA

The agora of Byllis was in the form of a regular rectangle, similar to agoras of the cities of Magna Graecia (Southern Italy). Its space was divided from the city by a decorative wall on the north and by the walls of the great stoa.

The agora was built sometime in the middle of the 3rd century BC according to a single plan that harmonized the theater, stoas, stadium, gymnasium and other public buildings. This was the place where political meetings were held and where festivals, theatrical performances, sporting events and religious ceremonies took place. The agora played the same role in the period of the Roman colony, when it was turned into the forum.

The entrance to the agora opened onto a perspective of the stairway of the stadium on the left, while on the right was the building of the ***prytaneion***, the office of the highest executive official of the *koinon*. The base of a statue was found in front of it, bearing a Latin inscription of the time of Augustus erected at the decision of the *decuriones* and under the care of the *duumviri*. Another inscription from the third century BC, dedicated to Artemis, came from the time of a *prytanis* with the Illyrian name of Triteutas.

To the west of the *prytaneion*, an environment without windows, perhaps an ***arsenal*** for weapons was built behind the wall of the

General view of agora. In the first plan- stoa A.

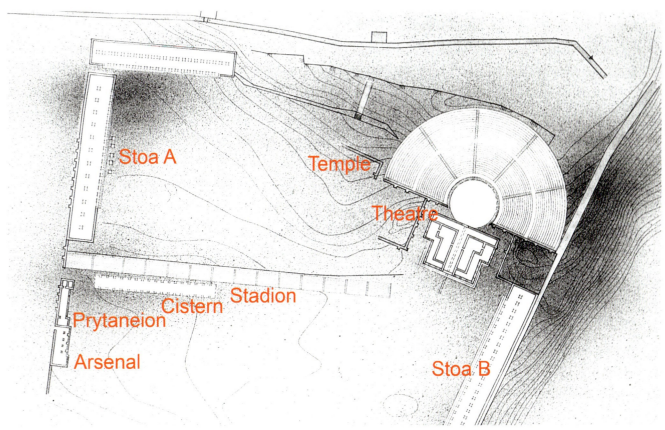

The agora of Byllis during 3rd – 2nd centuries BC (sketch).

Public building in the agora wall, possibly the arsenal, or the prison. Middle of the 3rd century BC.

ARCHAEOLOGICAL TREASURES FROM ALBANIA 31

Latin inscription on the basement of a statue with the names of the duumviri of the colony of Byllis. End of the 1st century BC.

Inscription dedicated to the goddess Artemis in the time of prytanis with the Illyrian name Triteutas.

Bronze coins of Byllis with the representation of the eagle, the serpent and the head of Zeus of Dodona. About 250 BC - 168 BC.

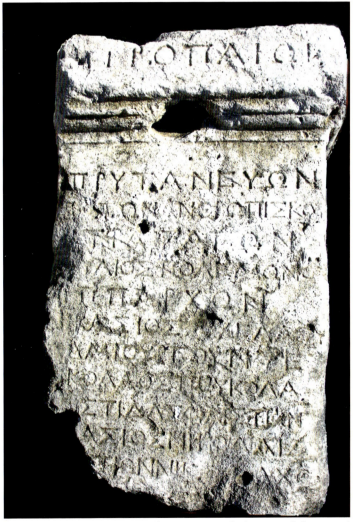

Inscription on the construction of a tropaion with the name of the prytanis Paton Anthropiskou, the strateg, the hypparchos and the damiorges of the Bylliones. End of the 3rd century BC.

Part of the frieze of the tropaion with the representation of a bucranion.

Relief of an Illyrian shield from the same monument.

Relief of the helmet of a Macedonian king from the same monument.

Architectonic element from the agora. 3rd – 2nd centuries BC.

View on the theatre of Byllis from its cavea.

The theatre of Byllis. General view from the west.

Ideal reconstruction of the frons scenae of the theatre in the middle of the 3rd century.

*Bronze token, used as a theatre ticket.
Second half of the 3rd century BC.*

Reconstructed part of the cavea of the theatre.

The stoa of the theatre.
Middle of the 3rd century BC.

*Comic actor playing the role of a slave seated on the altar of Dionysus.
Second half of the 3rd century BC.*

Eastern wing of the Great Stoa. Middle of the 3rd century BC.

Marble heads of the God Asclepius found in the stoa. 2nd century AD.

Eros. Local sculpture of the second half of the 3rd century BC, found in the Great Stoa.

Marble feet of a wooden sculpture (acroliths) found in the stoa. 2nd century AD.

Ideal reconstruction of the Great Stoa in the middle of the 3rd century.

agora. A row of octagonal columns supported the floor of the second story, which must have risen above the flat space of the agora. The space was rebuilt at the beginning of the first century AD.

The Theater

Together with the great stoa and the stadium, the theater determined the architectural composition of the agora from the middle of the third century BC. The theater loomed ahead as a majestic building, with the stage area in the front of the *cavea* (stairway). Two auxiliary supporting walls underlined this perspective, while the Doric colonnade of the portico of the stage created a monumental sense unknown for theaters of the time. According to a model also used in Dodona, the spectators crossed to the *parodoi*, which were embellished with decorative arches

In front of spectators, a low *proscenium* with an Ionian colonnade and an architrave with floral motifs held the platform on which the actors performed. Behind them rose the architectural background of the stage, with a Doric colonnade of which several column parts and the entablement are preserved. An altar stood in one corner of the orchestra. It shows an actor with a comic mask who has climbed onto the altar of Dionysus. The *cavea* of the theater has a diameter of 78 m giving 40 steps or seats, where 7,500 viewers could be seated. The theater of Byllis was also used in the period of the Roman colony, but it underwent a fundamental reconstruction.

A stoa built beside the theater, along the city wall, offered the spectators a place to relax. It was a construction two stories high, with a Doric colonnade in the lower story and an Ionian above.

The Stadium and the Cistern

Unlike the horseshow-shaped stadiums of other ancient cities, the stadium of Byllis has only one wing of nineteen steps, which is supported on the steeply sloping ground. The most notable particularity of the stadium of Byllis lies in the construction of a cistern of water under its northern wing. It was covered with a system of arches made of limestone blocks and collected water from the stairway of the stadium and from the roof of the great stoa. It was available to the many citizens who gathered in the agora during political activities, festivals, theatrical shows and sporting events.

A number of round bronze tokens bearing the inscription **Byllis** and serving as tickets for entry into the stadium or theatre were found. Bylline spectators kept them attached to their belts, since the clothing of the time did not have pockets.

The Great Stoa

The great *stoa* marked a boundary between the agora and the residential area in the north and the agora on the west, protecting its space from cold winds. It had the form of the letter L, with a total length of 144 m. It was built during the second quarter of the third century BC, adapting the Apollonian-Corinthian type, which had two stories, with a façade consisting of an Ionic colonnade over a Doric one.

The use of octagonal Doric columns is another adaptation from Apollonian architecture. The eastern part of the *stoa* is preserved in better condition, permitting a hypothetical reconstruction of the monument. Build around 270 BC, the *stoa* was still in use during the early period of the Roman colony. In the fifth century AD, basilica A was erected on the western side and some poor dwellings on the eastern wing of the *stoa*.

Streets and Dwellings

Byllis was built on *hypodamic* principles, that is, the surface area of the city was divided into a square network of roads or a grid. Four roads 8.30 m wide each, intersected every 69 m by side roads 6.60 m wide, creating *insulae* or square islands, made up the axis of this network.

The seats of the stadion. Middle of the 3rd century BC.

The head of Poseidon, found near the stadion. Local work in calcareous stone. Second half of the 3rd century BC.

The cistern under the stadion. Middle of the 3rd century BC.

View of dwelling A with peristile court. Middle of the 3rd century BC.

The peristile court of the dwelling B. Second half of the 3rd century BC.

Staircases carved in the rock in one of the streets of the city. Middle of the 3rd century BC.

Latin inscription on the southern rocks of Byllis, dedicated by the Roman veteran Marcus Lollianus, who built the road from the city to the region of Astacia. Middle of the 2nd century AD.

Marble portrait of Emperor Hadrian (117- 138 AD), found near the dwelling B.

Herm of a woman with the Illyrian name Mina and the typical Illyrian dress. Local work of the second half of the 3rd century BC.

Lamps of local production with the stamps of Italic firms Felix and Fortis.

Eros spanning the bow. Marble sculpture found in the Roman villa of Qesarat, near Byllis. First half of the 2nd century AD.

Latin inscription dedicated by Caius Iulius, a liberated slave of Augustus. About 30 BC.

Latin inscription dedicated to the emperor Antoninus Pius in 140 AD.

Latin grave inscription of the first half of the 1st century AD: "Caecilia, the daughter of Lucius from the tribe of Venusta, here is buried, together with her husband, Lartidius from Naissus, lived 42 years of holy life, without quarrels".

Each *insula* normally contained eight dwellings.

The dwelling A was excavated on the east side of the stoa and occupied an area of 30 x 24 m. A square courtyard, surrounded by a *peristyle* of the Ionic order, was the center of the composition of the rooms. In the southeast corner of the courtyard was the cistern, worked into the rock.

The dwelling A was built around the middle of the third century BC. During a reconstruction in the third century AD, the *andron* was paved with multi-colored mosaics in geometric patterns.

The dwelling B, measuring 29.5 x 24.8 m, was excavated on the western part of the city. It has also a rectangular courtyard, surrounded by a colonnade of the Doric order. A cistern was located in the southeast corner, collecting rainwater from the roof as a reserve for dry seasons. Built in third century BC, the residence kept the same function, up to the third century AD, when its walls were plastered and painted. A marble head of the Emperor Antoninus Pius (138-161 AD) was found near the northern walls of this residence.

Aerial view of Basilica A. In foreground: the agora wall; in background: the cistern of the stadium, the baths of Justinian and basilica C.

Basilica A. View from the East.

Panel of mosaic with the representation of birds and fishes in the central nave of Basilica A. First half of the 5th century AD.

Panel of mosaic with the representation of a lion in the central nave of Basilica A. First half of the 5th century AD.

BYZANTINE MONUMENTS

During the Byzantine period the grid system was abandoned. In its place, quarters grew up that were distinct from one another and grouped around the churches. Almost all of the monuments of the agora were destroyed and Victorinus used blocks of stones from them for the construction of the new wall.

The Cathedral (Basilica B)

The cathedral of Byllis, consisting of the basilica, baptistery and Episcopal complex, is the largest monument of the city in Late Antiquity. Its most important part took up an area of more than one hectare. The plan of the basilica in its final phase is characterized by a long and narrow structure, with side naves, narthex, exonarthex and the porticos of the atrium, crowned with galleries that increase its height considerably.

The floor of the exonarthex, the naves, the sanctuary and the northern wing of the transept were paved with mosaics, making this the largest surface covered with mosaics so far discovered in the territory of Albania. We find scenes from the daily life of shepherds, the lives of fishermen of Galilee, and the brothers Simon and Andrea. A great number of inscriptions on the floor of the central nave pertain in the largest part to repairs made during the period of Justinian.

All the walls were covered with frescos, but unfortunately, only those with geometric designs have been preserved. The Episcopal complex consisted of a large number of rooms, passages, courtyards, cisterns and monumental gates. The basilica was built at the end of the fourth century or the beginning of the fifth century AD, but destroyed during the Slavic invasions, around 547-551 AD.

Basilicas A, C, D, E

Basilica A was of monumental proportions, with a maximum length of 38.22 m and a maximum width of 23.42 m. The sanctuary, the central and northern naves and the narthex have floors paved with multi-colored mosaics. The motifs are varied, and some of them were original creations of the local atelier.

Basilica A was built in the first half of the fifth century and burnt during the Slavic invasions of the middle of the sixth century.

Basilica C is a church of average dimensions, 33 m long and 22.80 m wide. It had three naves, a narthex covered by a gallery, preceded by a portico, and several annexes.

The sanctuary and one of the annexes are paved with mosaics. In one, two flocks of six lambs each, personifying the twelve apostles, go toward the altar. In the second, members of the clergy carrying candelabra in their hands head for church An inscription written on the mosaic tells that it was made in the time of Bishop Praisios. Basilica C seems to have been built in the second quarter of the sixth century AD.

Basilica D was excavated in the northern part of the city, outside the wall of Victorinus. Its entrance is located on the west, with a simple *propylaeon*, an atrium with four porticos and a *narthex* that connects to the two rooms north and south of it.

Basilica D stands out for the good quality of its floor mosaics. Among the scenes is one of the Rivers of Paradise: *Pishon, Gihon, Tigris* and *Euphrates*. It was built at the beginning of the sixth century AD.

Basilica E has been excavated outside the Victorinus wall, on the eastern side of the ancient city. It is 33 m long and 22.80 m wide, with the floor of the sanctuary paved with mosaics.

The Byzantine City Walls

With its central location Byllis remained an important city for the province of New Epirus. The ancient surrounding walls of Byllis were re-fortified after the destruction that the city suffered from Gothic onslaughts at the beginning of the 5th century AD.

After the destruction of the city by the Slavs in 547-551 AD, Justinian

Aerial view of Basilica B. In background the wall of Victorinus.

General view of Basilica B.

ARCHAEOLOGICAL TREASURES FROM ALBANIA 57

The central nave of Basilica B.

View of Basilica B from the East.

The atrium of Basilica B and the colonnade of the quadriporticus.

The exonarthex of Basilica B.

Scene of fishing in the mosaic of the exonarthex: Saint Peter and Saint Andrew as fisherman.

View through the exonarthex of the basilica.

*Fragments from the mosaic of the exonarthex:
The shepherd, the dog watching over the sheep and the wolf approaching the flock.*

*Bucolic scene in the mosaic of the exonarthex.
Second half of the 5th century AD.*

*Tribelon in the baptisterium of Basilica B.
Second half of the 5th century AD.*

Aerial view of Basilica C.

View of Basilica C from the East.

The central nave of Basilica C. View from the West.

The capital of tribelon in the central nave of Basilica C. About 530 AD.

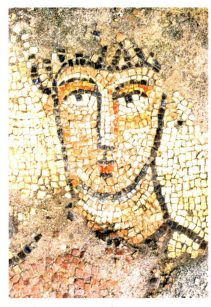
Basilica C. Human figure in the mosaic of the altar.

Fig. a-d: The mosaics of Basilica C. About 530 AD. The sheep as symbol of apostles and the birds.

Fig. e-f: The dog and the rabbit. Fragments of Basilica E.

Aerial view of Basilica D.

The deer. Mosaic from the central nave of Basilica D. Beginning of 6th century AD.

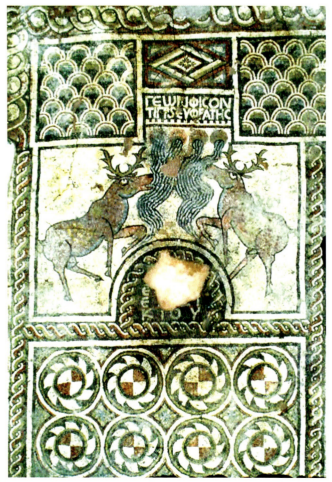

Deer drinking water from the rivers of Paradise: Geon, Fison, Tigris and Euphrates. Mosaic from the central nave of Basilica D.

The doplphins. Mosaic from the central nave of Basilica E.

View of Basilica D from the wall of Victorinus.

Aerial view of Basilica E.

Aerial view of the castle built by Victorinus in Byllis. About 530 AD.

ordered the construction of surrounding walls. The inscriptions tell us, it was Victorinus who was in charge. Along the entire western and southern sides of the city, he used the walls of the ancient periods, while on the north and east, he built a new wall 2.20 m thick, with six three-story towers each 12 m high. One part of the south-west wall was built with *spolia* from the theater, and a large number of seats from the theater can be distinguished.

THE BATHS OF JUSTINIAN

The cistern under the stadion continued in use until the Byzantine period. Public baths were erected west of it, taking advantage of its water. Its structure contents: the *apodyterium* (dressing room), *frigidarium* (cold water baths), *tepidarium* (warm room), *sudatio* (sweat bath), *caldarium* (hot room), and *praefurnum* (oven and fire room). An inscription, found in the city, speaks of the construction of baths in the time of Justinian I.

Staircases to the guard's path.

The tower in the south-east corner of the castle.

Seats from the theatre and blocks with inscriptions, reused in the construction of the south-east tower.

View on the wall Victorinus from basilica B.

Justinian's baths near the cistern of the ancient stadion.

THE BASILICA OF BALLSH

The ruins of the basilica in the city of Ballsh, together with the other ruins around it, are known as the Monastery of St. Mary. The basilica of Ballsh, built in the period of Justinian, had the exonarthex, the narthex, three naves and a baptistery, later transformed into a chapel. The many similarities with the basilica of Byllis help determine the time of its construction to have been the second quarter of the 6th century AD. The basilica of Ballsh was entirely rebuilt in the 9th century, reusing much *spolia* taken from the city of Byllis, including the inscriptions of Victorinus. An inscription found in the ruins of the church of Ballsh during the First World War speaks on the converting of Boris and the Bulgarian people to the Christian faith in the ninth century (864 AD). In written sources in the Greek and Bulgarian languages Ballsh is known as Kefalenia, or Glavinica, a translation from the Albanian word *ballë*, meaning forehead.

Lintels from the main gate of basilica B of Byllis, reused in the basilica of Ballsh. About 530 AD.

View of the basilica of Ballsh.

ANCIENT SETTLEMENTS AROUND BYLLIS

KLOS (NIKAIA)

The ancient city of Klos was built during the second half of fifth century BC on a hill steeply sloping on three sides, connected by a pass with the hill on which Byllis rose. The surrounding wall, 1850 m long, completely circles the hill over an area of 18 hectares.

Although it was only one kilometer from Byllis, Nikaia preserved a special political and social life, as it is shown by the construction of its own agora in the 3rd century BC. Besides the theater and a stoa that has been excavated, the traces of a stadium appear in the agora, with a one-sided setting as in Byllis. This was just the period when a young man from Nikaia won a competition in armed running in the games of the city Oropos (Beotia) in Greece.

The theater of Klos, like that of Byllis, has reached our days extremely damaged. Of the stairway, only the first step, the *proedria*, is well preserved. From 800 to 1,000 spectators could fit in its seating area, with 15 rows.

Fourteen decrees of the second half of 3rd century BC, on the grant

View on the hill of Klos.

The surrounding wall of the ancient city in Klos. Second half of the 5th century BC.

repeats the model of Phoenice. The walls were built with limestone blocks only for the *krepis*, with bricks over them, according to the Apollonian model. The area within the surrounding walls is full of ancient residences, set on terraces in a grid system. Archaeological data show that the city had an intensive life, especially in the third century BC, when the Illyrian King Monunius, who subjugated Dyrrhachion and Apollonia around 280 BC, established his residence in Gurëzeza.

Some local sculptures, founded occasionally in the necropolis, are from a high quality. In a lime stone stele of third century BC, two women are preparing for a ceremony at the cemetery, on a commemorative day that would coincide with that of the Pentecost. The clothing of the women and the presence of a slave testify to the high social standing of the persons who ordered this relief to be built.

A bronze tablet of the first half of the second century BC, found in the hinterland of Apollonia, seems to come from Gurëzeza. It was once exhibited in a square in a center of the *koinon* of the Balaites, perhaps the same city of Gurëzeza. Translated from ancient Greek, the inscription says:

"When Bion, son of Kleigeneas was *prytanis,* on the eighteenth day in the month of Psidreos, the *tamias* Aristen, son of Eksakios reported to the Council of Elders and the *Ecclesia* that inasmuch as the *peripolarchos* Aristen, son of Parmen has done good things and even more for the Balaites, it seemed right to the Balaites to crown the *peripolarchos*

Ancient cistern in Gurezeza. 4th century BC.

Aristen, son of Parmen with a golden crown of five *hryseis* for his merits. And the *peripolarchos* Aristen, son of Parmen, thanking the Balaites for the privileges that they gave him, crowns the *koinon* of the Balaites with the same crown. The Balaites judged it right that the decision be engraved on a bronze plaque and put in a visible place, for the good things previously done by him. Even the children shall benefit from the general rights. And the *gramatei* Parmen, son of Teisarchos and Bulos, son of Abaios shall also enjoy the rights."

The plaque was a joint decree of a meeting of the people and the elders of the *koinon* of the Balaites. From his name, it appears that the *peripolarchos* Aristen, son of Parmen was the commander of the border guards of Apollonia.

The archaeological data testify that the ancient city of Gurëzeza was destroyed during the campaign of Paullus Aemilius in 167 BC and was not rebuilt until Middle Ages.

THE ANCIENT CITY OF MARGËLLIÇ

The hill of the castle of Margëlliç is distinguished by its pyramidal form in the range of hills that separates the plain of Myzeqe from the valley of the Gjanica. In the second half of the 4th century BC a surrounding wall of the Apollonian type, with a *krepis* of the quadratic lime stone blocks and bricks over it, was built.

Although it was a relatively small urban settlement, perhaps the city of Bargullum, ancient Margëlliç had an internal spatial organization based on the orthogonal or grid system. Roads 3 to 3.55 m wide were paved with sandstone slabs, while smaller roads 1.2 m wide bordered residences.

Like Klos and Gurëzeza, the ancient city of Margëlliç was destroyed during the campaign of Paullus Aemilius in 167 BC. A terracotta of Aphrodite *Antheia* (Aphrodite of the flowers of spring), 44.5 high, produced in Apollonia, was found during the excavation of a residence in Margëlliç. With its perfected artistic treatment and large dimensions, it constitutes a true work of art of the 3rd century BC.

During Late Antiquity, only the highest part of the hill was re-fortified in the same building technique as that of the fortifications of Victorinus in Byllis.

Street of the 3rd – 2nd centuries BC, discovered during the archaeological excavations in the Illyrian city of Margëlliç.

Aphrodite. Terracotta of Apollonian production, found in Margëlliç. First half of the 2nd century BC.

Agricultural iron tools found in Margëlliç. First half of the 2nd century BC.

Grave stele of Parmeniskos Ieronos, found in Margëlliç. 3rd century BC.

82 Byllis

Head of a girl. Local work in calcareous stone.
3rd century BC

AMANTIA

Situated on a rocky plateau with an area of 13 hectares and protected naturally from major rock falls, Amantia had a proto-urban beginning. This is shown by archaic bronzes belonging to the 6th century BC. Around the middle of the 5th century BC, Amantia assumed the form of a real city, at least in its exterior appearance. A wall 2,100 meters long surrounded the whole plateau on which the settlement extended, running to the edge of the ravines.

The city had three entrances and a number of bastions that helped provide a focus for the defence of the long walls. Amantia's wall, built with a polygonal technique like that of Klos and Buthrotum, would remain the model of a perfect work through many later centuries. Such an enterprise could have been achieved only by a

View toward Amantia from the territory of the Bylliones.

Part of the surrounding wall of Amantia. About 450 BC.

civic community that had assembled the necessary financial means and which had qualified craftsmen at its disposition. The castle of Matohasanaj also belongs to this community. It was built at the same time as Amantia, some 14 kilometers to the east, to control the entrance from the east into the territory of the Amantes, which stretched out along the left bank of the river Aoos (Vjosa). In a second period, construction with rectangular isodomic blocks is dated to the middle of the fourth century BC. Amantia was also re-fortified during the reign of Justinian I (527-565 AD).

The Stadium. The best preserved monument is the stadium. Its stone rows, set in the form of an extended horseshoe, followed a track 12.5 meters wide and about 60 meters long. On one side, supported by the face of a hill, were 17 rows, while on the other side, built over an infill of earth, there were only eight rows.

The Temple. On the south side of the city, outside the walls, an ancient temple has been discovered. It was a *peripter* of the Doric order, with dimensions of 12.5 x 6.75 meters. A marble sculpture of a supine woman, perhaps the symbol of a river, comes from its pediment. Several dedicatory inscriptions that have been found, as well as an inscription describing the reconstruction of a temple of Aphrodite, appear to be linked with just this temple.

The temple, built in the third century BC, continued to be used up to the first centuries AD. During Late Antiquity, an early Christian basilica was built near the ruins of the temple, using its materials. The basilica had three naves divided by arcades erected over columns, a narthex and annexes. Amantia is shown to have been a bishopric since 344 AD, when bishop Eulalius took part in the council of Philippopolis.

The south-east gate of Amantia. First half of the 4th century BC.

View of the acropolis of Amantia. In the foreground – the stadium.

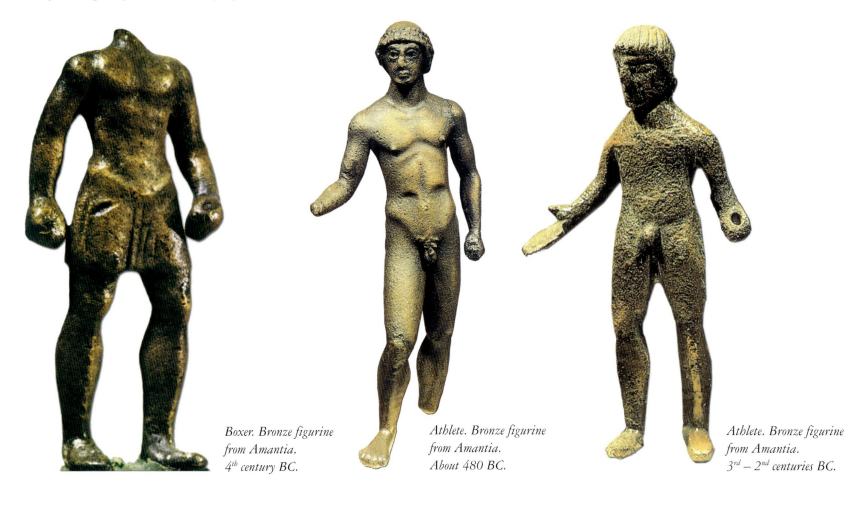

Boxer. Bronze figurine from Amantia. 4th century BC.

Athlete. Bronze figurine from Amantia. About 480 BC.

Athlete. Bronze figurine from Amantia. 3rd – 2nd centuries BC.

The stadium of Amantia. First half of the 3rd century BC.

Kouros. Head of a bronze figurine from Amantia. About 520 BC.

Excavations in the stadium of Amantia. 1954.

Amantia

Temple of Aphrodite and the paleochristian basilica. View from the acropolis of Amantia.

The river Aoos represented as a reclining girl. Marble sculpture from the pediment of the Aphrodite temple. 3rd century BC.

Bronze coins of Amantia with a representation of Zeus and the thunderbolt. 3rd century BC.

The local god of prosperity in the company of the nymphs. Stone relief of the 3rd century BC.

Dog. Bronze figurine found in Amantia. 3rd – 2nd centuries BC

Ram. Bronze figurine from Amantia. 3rd – 2nd centuries BC.

The surrounding wall of the ancient city of Olympe. Beginning of the 4th century BC.

The second surrounding wall of Olympe. Middle of the 4th century BC.

OLYMPE

The ancient author Stephen of Byzantium mentions an Illyrian city named Olympe but says nothing more. Its identification became possible from the large-scale finds of its coins in the ruins of the ancient city in the village of Mavrovë in the Vlora district.

The ancient city stretched out between the two summits of a hill and along its western slope. Two periods of construction can be distinguished in the city's fortifications, by the different lines of the walls. The first encloses only the southern part of the hill, leaving open the part that is impassable before of rock falls. A bastion with a front wall of 6,60 m is well preserved, built of large rectangular blocks with unpolished faces, quite similar to the surrounding wall of the second half of the 5th century BC in Klos.

The second encirclement included a surface twice as large, about 16 ha, with a wall 1500 m long. The surrounding wall, 3,30 m wide, is an *emplekton* of the rectangular isodomic type, with regular rows of an equal height of 0,60 m (two feet). It dates from around the middle of the 4th century BC.

Several graves from the city's necropolis have been excavated. They were cist graves, of large limestone tiles, the same as in Amantia. The inventory is relatively rich, with the use of large amphorae produced specifically for this purpose, as well as coins from Apollonia of the 3rd - 2nd BC.

It was proven from archaeological excavations that the beginning of life in the city dates to the 6th century BC, before the construction of the first fortification. The city flourished in the 3rd – 2nd centuries BC, when Olympe even coined its own bronze money. An interesting category is represented by the large amphorae produced in the city, which have a local interpretation of the form as well as an embellishment that is quite formal, with red figures or application of reliefs.

Olympe was the centre of an autonomous *koinon*, as shown by an inscription of the second half of the third century BC, which mentions as the main civil servants the *politarchos*, four *synarchontes* and a secretary.

Urban life was interrupted in Olympe during the 1st century BC, when the centre of the region developed more in Aulona (Vlora).

Bronze coins of Olympe with a representation of Zeus and the thunderbolt. 3rd century BC.

The mosaic of the northern nave of the basilica of Mesaplik, near Amantia.
First half of the 6th century BC.

*Grave stele of Onesima, who lived to be 16. 3rd century AD.
From Drashovica, near Amantia*

96 AULONA (VLORA)

Woman with Illyrian dress, known as "The Maiden of Vlora". Calcareous stone sculpture from Aulona. First half of the 3rd century BC.

Calcareous stone herm of Fingeia in Illyrian dress. Aulona, 2nd - 1st century BC.

Calcareous stone stele representing a religious ceremony. End of the 5th century BC.

AULONA (VLORA)

Aulona is mentioned for the first time in the historical sources in the first half of the 2nd century AD by Lucian (Nav. 7), who places it in the land of the Chelydonians or the Taulantes. At the same period, the geographer Ptolemy Alexander (III, 12, 2) called Aulona the city of the Taulantes. The origin of the name seems to be Liburnian, and the traces of habitation are the most ancient.

At the one-time site of the port, which was found in the vicinity of today's Flag Square (Sheshi i Flamurit), a relief of the 5th century BC has been found. It is apparently from ancient Aulona that the sculpture of a girl in Illyrian dress, known as the Maiden of Vlora, originates.

The city took on real development only in the 1st – 2nd centuries AD, in the role of a road station on the way from Apollonia to Buthrotum (Butrint). In the 4th century BC, the city was surrounded with a rectangular castle, the walls of which have been discovered behind the Independence Monument.

Sunset in the Bay of Vlora. From left to right: the peninsula of Karaburun (Acroceraunia), the island of Sazan (Sason) and the Cape of Treport.

KANINA

The surrounding walls of the medieval fortification of today's Kanina were built throughout all their length over the foundations of an Illyrian castle with an area of about 3,6 ha. The well-preserved parts on the southern and north-eastern sides show a technique the same as that of the walls of Apollonia or Treport from the middle of the 4th century BC. They were built with rectangular blocks that form a *krepis*, on which a brick wall rises. Archaeological excavations show that the castle of Kanina was built around the middle of the 4th century BC and flourished in the 3rd – 2nd centuries BC, when it provided an outlet to the sea for the *koinon* of the Amantes.

The development of the harbour and the road station of Aulona in the 1st century AD caused the castle to lose its importance, but it became valued again as an important fortification during Late Antiquity.

View toward the castle of Kanina and the Bay of Vlora from the mountain of Shushica.

TREPORT

The cape of Treport, which closes the bay of Vlora from the north, was the *acropolis* of a large Illyrian city in antiquity. The *acropolis* itself was created during the $6^{th} - 5^{th}$ centuries BC as a proto-urban centre, while in the 4th BC, a genuine city that spread over 30 ha was built up.

In the bay of Treport, when the tide is out, the west wing of a surrounding wall can be seen for about 800 m, covered at high tide by the surface of the sea. It was constructed with rectangular blocks in the form of a *krepis* on which a wall of bricks was erected, as in Apollonia.

Archaeological excavations have shown that the city flourished during the 4th to 2nd Centuries BC and was abandoned in the 1st century BC. Its strategic position in the Bay of Vlora, which belonged to the Taulantes in the 4th century BC, as well as the size of the city, testifies that it was an important city, not yet identified.

Traces of the surrounding wall of the ancient city of Treport, covered by the sea. Photo of Luigi M. Ugolini (1924).

ORICUM

Oricum is located in the southernmost recess of the Bay of Vlora, at the edge of the mountains of Karaburun (the Acroceraunian Mountains). According to legend, it was founded by warriors from Euboea returning from the Trojan War, but archaeological data show that it was founded from Corinth and Corfu, right after Apollonia. That it coined its own bronze coins, shows that Oricum was an independent city during the $3^{rd} - 1^{st}$ centuries BC.

The hill of Paleokastra over which the city extends is quite low, 20 m in height, and not protected by nature. According to Livy (XXIX, 40, 3), in 214 BC Philip V of Macedonia "conquered it at the first attack, because the city was in a flat place and did not have strong walls." In 48 BC, the city was surrendered without a fight to Julius Caesar in the civil war with Pompey, but a few months later, it resisted a siege from land and sea by Pompey son. Even after those events, Oricum remained a free city and was not turned into a Roman colony.

The traces of a surrounding wall with a circumference of about 950 m, which encircled the hill where its slopes met flat land, show two periods of construction. The first one is represented by sections with a width of 3.50 m, made of polished limestone blocks in a right-angled form, placed in horizontal rows. The second period, belonging to Late

View from the hill of Oricum toward the bay and the lagoon.

View over the Bay of Oricum from the mountain of Shashica.

The theatre of Oricum; built in the middle of the 3rd century BC and reconstructed in the 1st century AD.

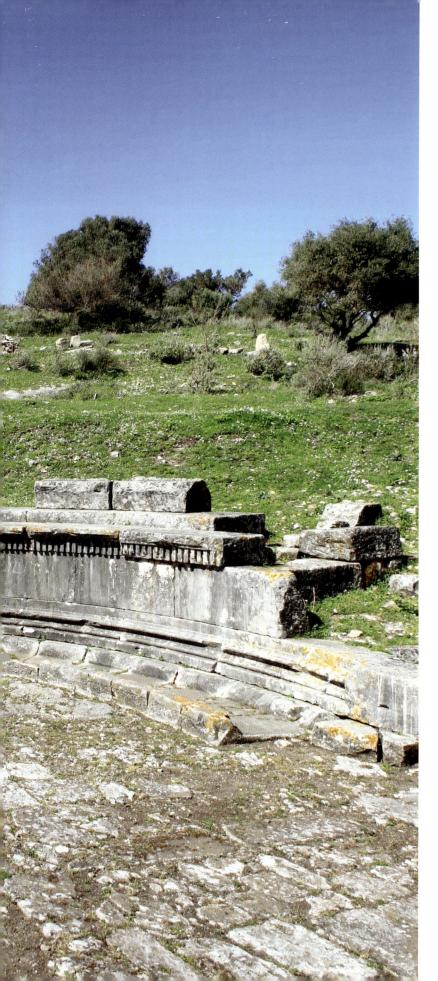

Antiquity, is represented by a reconstruction 1.80 m wide, made with stone and mortar. Part of it, on the south side, is below the level of the lagoon today, because the level of the sea has risen since ancient times.

The city's *agora* was located on its eastern side, where the theatre was discovered. A *conistra* of the Roman period has survived, as well as the orchestra with a diameter of 9.40 m, which is laid with stone tiles. Several seats of the *proedria* have also been found, with arm rests decorated with the paws of a sphinx. Traces of etchings on the rock in back are evidence that the *cavea* rested on it and an artificial landfill, while the seats were made of stone blocks.

Based on what remains, it can be calculated that the theatre had a capacity of about 600 spectators.

Traces on the rock permit us to understand that the residential sections of the city were laid out according to an orthogonal network oriented according to the points of the horizon. A few metres above the theatre, one of the city's roads begins. It is 2.40 m wide, etched in the rock in the form of a stairway.

The economy of the city was mainly tied to the exploitation of fishing in the lagoon of Dukat, wood from the Acroceraunian Mountains and for building ships, and also rock quarries. The latter are found at the seacoast, to the north of the city, and served to furnish the buildings of Apollonia and Dyrrhachium with limestone blocks or columns. The largest quarry was found on the western shoreline of the Acroceraunian peninsula, in Gramma Bay, which served as a refuge for ships caught by storms while passing through the Otranto Channel. The name comes from the numerous inscriptions etched during antiquity and the Middle Ages by sailors sheltered there. The quarry was used since the archaic period, but the earliest inscriptions belong to the $3^{rd} - 2^{nd}$ centuries BC. Several of them are dedicated to the Dioscuri, protectors of sailors.

Oricum. Street carved in the rock. 4th century BC.

GRAMMA

The quarries in the Acroceraunian Mountains (the peninsula of Karaburun) were one of the main sources of the wealth of Oricum, providing large blocks for the construction of monuments. They continued to be exploited during the Imperial Roman period, which can be seen by blocks found in several monuments of Apollonia and Dyrrhachion. However, such use was limited, and the quarries were abandoned by the end of the 3rd century AD, depriving Oricum of one of its principal means of sustenance. The largest of these quarries was located on the western coast of the Karaburun peninsula, in a bay protected from the waves of the sea. Today this bay is called Gramma (from the Greek word for letter), because of the numerous inscriptions left by sailors who found shelter there during storms. The earliest of these inscriptions belong to the 3rd-2nd centuries BC, but they continue also into Roman and Byzantine times. Among those who wrote on the face of the cliffs, the names of Sulla and Pompey Junior can be made out.

View of Gramma Bay. The former bed of the ancient quarries can be made out under the water.

Gramma Bay, on the stormy shore of the Acroceraunian peninsula.

Ancient quarries in the Gramma bay.

Ancient inscriptions on the rock face in Gramma Bay.

Latin inscription with the name of Gneius Pompey.

One of the faces of the ancient quarry covered by inscriptions of the 3rd century BC - 1st century AD.

PALASA (PALESTE)

In 5th of January of 48 BC, Caesar set sail in bad weather from Brindisium at the head of seven legions (42,000 soldiers) with the other part of the fleet. He did this to avoid the mightier navy of Pompey, which controlled the Adriatic coast. The next day he landed in Paleste (present day Palasa) on the coast of the Germini, which is north of Himara and near the present day village of Dhërmi. After a forced march over the Acroceraunian Mountains, he seized Oricum. This sudden success forced Apollonia to succumb without a fight, and the Byllines, Amantes and Epirotes swore fealty and obedience.

When Pompey learned of Caesar's landing, he was in Candavia (Babja of Librazhd), coming down with his army along the Via Egnatia from Macedonia to Dyrrhachion, where he had planned to spend the winter. Trying to keep the initiative, he sent his son to Oricum at the head of the Egyptian fleet, and Caesar's garrison was caught by surprise. Most of the Cesar's ships lying at anchor in the inner port, which is a lagoon today, were burned.

Some months later Pompey decided to attack his opponent's camp near Petra of Dyrrhachion by surprise. His men disembarked from ships and went into the depths of the defensive lines, took the fortifications and put Caesar's army to flight. Leaving 960 of his men dead on the field of battle, Caesar withdrew in good order through the Aous valley into Macedonia. Pompey headed in the same direction, by but a shorter route along the Via Egnatia through Candavia.

The decisive battle between the two armies took place in Pharsala of Thessaly, where Caesar resoundingly defeated his opponent, paving the way for the age of autocratic rule in Rome.

View from the place known as the "Camp of Caesar" toward the Bay of Oricum.

View of the coast of Palasa - ancient Palaeste, where Caesar landed with his army in his campaign against Pompey in 48 BC. The line of the ancient road can be made out on the facing slope of the mountain.

Typical dwelling in the village of Dukat, near Oricum. 18th century.

Part of the Roman road of Acroceraunia. 2nd century AD.

HIMARA and BORSH

In antiquity, the seacoast of Himara is associated with the tribe of the Argyrini, who lived in the forested Acroceraunian Mountains, according to Stephen of Byzantium. During the 4th century BC, this area was included in the *koinon* of the Chaonians, but during the 3rd – 2nd centuries BC, it appears to have been divided into two separate autonomous regions, one around Himara and the other around Borsh.

Himara is mentioned by Pliny, under the name Himera (NH, IV, 1), as one of the castles of Epirus in the Acroceraunians. In an inscription of the 2nd century BC, it appears as the centre of an autonomous *koinon* that is invited to take part in the festivals of Delphi, along with Phoenice and Amantia.

The castle extending under today's residential area is dated to the first half of the 4th century BC, from the wall technique that is similar to

The castle of Himara, after Edward Lear (1851).

View of Castle of Himara and the Bay of Spile.

Bastion of the 4th century BC of the ancient Castle of Himara, reconstructed in the 6th century AD.

Streets in the Castle of Himara.

Frieze of an ancient monument in the window of a house in the Castle of Himara. 3rd century BC.

View from the Castle of Himara towards the Bay of Limion.

that of Butrint and Phoenice. The walls run for more than 100 m to the northeast, where a bastion is preserved with a facade 6,3 m high, constructed with large limestone blocks in rectangular and polygonal forms. The frieze of a monument of the 3rd – 2nd century BC is embedded in the walls of a residence. In addition, during soundings the base of a *stoa* from the same period has been found, testifying to the presence of an *agora*.

Reconstructions with stone and mortar over the ancient wall belong to the period of Late Antiquity, when Himara figures among the castles of Old Epirus (Epirus Vetus), rebuilt by Emperor Justinian.

The castle of Borsh coincides with the Spring of the King's Water mentioned by Pliny. The ancient fortification, known as the castle of Sopot, encircled the top of a hill and had a surface area of 2,5 ha. The surrounding wall can be followed along the whole western face, where there are some well-preserved sections made of rectangular blocks. The similarity to the fortifications of Himara, Phoenice and Butrint place its construction to the first half of the 4th century BC. There is also a second enclosure that created an *acropolis* on the highest part of the hill. The ruins of residences, built with rectangular blocks, can be distinguished in the area within the walls. On the western side of the castle, near the surrounding wall, a monumental grave in the form of a chamber, constructed with rectangular blocks, has been discovered. The natural port of Palermo served both the castle of Himara and that of Borsh in antiquity.

There are no ancient traces on the small peninsula jutting out into the port or on its shores, but underwater archaeological research has discovered numerous ceramic pieces of the ancient period, testifying to the use of the bay in Antiquity.

View of the Castle of Borsh.

The Castle of Borsh.
The surrounding wall on the eastern slope.

*The surrounding wall in the western slope.
First half of the 4th century BC.*

*Monumental tomb in the ancient necropolis of the castle.
Second half of the 3rd century BC.*

View from the Castle of Borsh toward the Ionian Sea.

View of the Castle of Ali Pasha in the Bay of Palerm.

The Eastern Tower of the castle.

Eucharistia. Scene on the mosaic of the basilica of Onchesmus. 6th century AD.

ONCHESMUS (SARANDA)

Onchesmus (Saranda) was first mentioned by Strabo in the 1st century BC, when it seemed to serve as a harbour for Phoenice. Archaeological finds indicate that Onchesmus developed into a city on its own as early as the 2nd century AD, and was fortified in the 6th century AD. What are left of this centre today are the walls of the rectangular castle, with one face constructed straight on the sea-shore. In the early part of the 6th century AD Onchesmus was one of the principal cities in the province of Old Epirus, and an archivescoval centre.

A synagogue, adapted to a palaeochristian basilica was uncovered within the enclosure of the castle. The nave multicoloured mosaics, showing a menorah and scenes of two stags flanking a cantharus, are assigned to the 5-6th century AD. The actual name of Saranda is derived from the Byzantine church of Forty Saints (saranda-forty in Greek), situated near the Gjashta Pass. The recent excavations on the south side of narthex discovered the entrance to a chambered crypt system, in which some wall paintings survive.

The synagogue of Onchesmus, transformed into a paleochristian basilica during the 6th century AD.

132 Onchesmus (Saranda)

Part of the surrounding wall of Onchesmus in the bay of Saranda.

Arch from the crypt of Forty Saints' basilica in Saranda. 6th century AD.

Forty Saints' basilica in Saranda. View from the east.

Underground rooms in the Forty Saints' basilica in Saranda.

PHOENICE

In Polibius's words, Phoenice, was the most highly fortified and richest city of Epirus. It became also its capital in 231-167 BC. The city was established on top a 270-m high hill. A 3-km long wall encompassed nearly the whole of its western slope stretching over an area of 40 hectares.

During 1926-1927, L. M. Ugolini carried out excavations on the circuit-wall, and discovered several monuments. Thesauros, a small sanctuary for ceremonies or meetings, was the most important amongst them. In the last years, Albanian-Italian excavations uncovered a part of a city quarter, including a Hellenistic building with a peristyle courtyard decorated with Ionic colonnades and the scene of the theatre.

The tent of L. M. Ugolini during his excavations in Phoenice, 1926-1927.

View of the hill of Phoenice.

Enormous stone blocks in the surrounding wall of Phoenice. Beginning of the 4th century BC.

Excavated orchestra of the theatre of Phoenice. 3rd century BC.

Marble female heads found in Phoenice.

Marble statue of Artemis. 3rd century BC.　　*Marble statue of Artemis. 2nd century AD.*

MESOPOTAM

The Monastery of Mesopotam, set up on top a hill surrounded by the Bistrica waters, was also connected to mediaeval Butrint. The Saint Nicholas Church is established at the centre of the enclosure. What made this church peculiar for the time are the two apses at its east end, accounted for by the reverence shown for two saints (Saint Nicholas and Saint Mary), or two religions, Orthodox and Catholic. Evidence of this are also the three lilies (a symbol of the Angevin dynasty) decorating the narthex floor, which can only be explained by the fact that the church was built at the time when Buthrotum was held by the Catholic Angevins (1272-1286). A large number of relieves depicting monsters, which were cut into the blocks of the church outer wall, are assigned to this period.

The eastern wall of the church of the Monastery of Mesopotam, built with spolia from the ancient monuments of Phoenice.

The church of the Monastery of Mesopotam. 13th century.

Reliefs of monsters on the walls of the church of the Monastery of Mesopotam. 13th century.

BUTHROTUM

HISTORY

According to legend, Buthrotum was founded by Helenus, the son of Priam, King of Troy who was being held captive by Neoptolemus, son of Achilles. Following the latter's death, Helenus had became king, and had married to Hector's window, Andromache. En route from Troy, Aeneas paid a visit to Buthrotum where found his Trojan compatriots:

> *I saw before me Troy in miniature*
> *................................ and I pressed*
> *My body against a Scaean Gate. Those with me*
> *Feasted their eyes on this, our kinsmen's town.*
> *In spacious colonnades the king received them,*
> *And offering mid-court their cups of wine*
> *They made libation, while on plates of gold*
> *A feast was brought before them.*

(Virgil, *Aeneid,* III)

No scientific evidence has been produced in support of this legend and archaeological excavations have revealed that, during the 12th century BC Trojan exodus Buthrotum was just a fishermen's village. The city was recorded for the first time by the Greek geographer Hecataeus of Miletus in the 6th century BC.

At that time Buthrotum was a small acropolis under Corcyrean control. The main entrance unearthed south to the fortification leads off to a sanctuary, to which belongs the relief of a lion devouring a bull's head. Several architectonic sections, as well as a number of ceramic fragments with dedicatory inscriptions on them is what remains of it. The situation in the Corcyrian emporion of Buthrotum changed radically at the turn of the 4th century BC, when the Molossian king Alketas invaded the coasts opposite Corcyra, Chaonia inclusive. Buthrotum changed from an *emporion* into a fortified city, where the

Virgil between two muses.
Roman mosaic of the 2nd century AD.

old fortification was conserved as an acropolis. During the last decades of the 4th century BC, the chief tribes in Epirus, the Molossians, Thesprotians and Chaonians, created the *Symmachy* of Epirus, a military alliance run by the Aeachidian kings, with wide autonomy being granted to the regions. Phoenice became the Chaonias' capital city and Buthrotum the center of the Prasaebes Koinon, one of the autonomous subdivisions of the Chaonians. Inscriptions indicate that the *strategus*, a military leader, was the highest official in the koinon. He was aided by the *prostates*, the representative of the Chaonians'

Archaeological sites of Chaonia.

central authority. The priest of Asclepius, elected annually like the rest of the officials, occupied an important place in this hierarchy.

In 231 BC, as a consequence of an uprising, the monarchy in Epirus was brought down, and the republic known as the Epirotes' Koinon, based in Phoenice, was declared. The Prasaebes Koinon, with Buthrotum as its centre, remained an autonomous territory in the Epirotes' Koinon until 167 BC, when Consul Aemilius Paullus's Roman army devastated Molossia and other Epirote provinces. Thanks to its relations with Rome, Chaonia was not affected by this destruction.

Due to its favourable location, Buthrotum had also a role to play in the 49-48 BC civil war, serving as a base for Caesar's army. It was Augustus who, around 30 BC, establish a Roman settlement in Buthrotum through. As compared to other cities under the Roman Empire, Buthrotum remained a minor centre, but an important road-station on the way from Aulona, across the Acroceraunia Mountains and Phoenice, on to Nicopolis.

During the 5th and early 6th century AD Buthrotum emerges as an early archivescoval centre under the Nicopolis metropolis, too. The city walls were reconstructed and an archivescoval palace, the baptistery and the basilica represent high-level technical constructions, which speak of the prevailing state of prosperity and security in Buthrotum.

Archaeological finds prove that during the early Middle Ages Buthrotum was not abandoned. In the 9th century, the city was under Byzantine domination and its Bishopric found itself under Naupact metropolis. In 1081, Buthrotum was captured by Boemund, the son of the Norman King Robert Guiscard. In an attempt to gain control over Corcyra and the Straits, three years later both of them lost a sea battle to the Byzantines and Venetians just in front of the city.

Over the 11th-14th centuries, Buthrotum fell in the hands of different Norman, Epirote, Sueve, and Angevin rulers. After the 4th crusade (1204) the city had joined the Despotate of Epirus, created by the Byzantine General Michael Angelos Comnenus. Buthrotum had all the way until 1257 been under the constant domination of the Epirote despots.

In 1272, Buthrotum was taken by the King of Sicily Charles of Anjou who created the Kingdom of Albania (*Regnum Albaniae*), encompassing the entire maritime Albania as far north as Durrës, only to be surrendered to the Venetians in 1386. Throughout this period Buthrotum saw a period of genuine flourishing, with strong fortifications being laid out on the acropolis, and on the north-facing hillside where the life of the city had been removed.

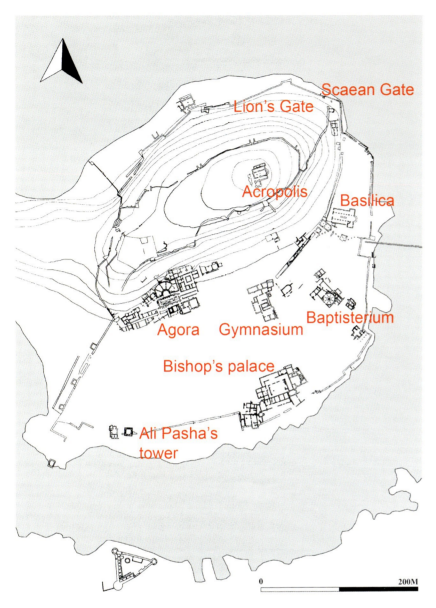

Plan of ancient Butrint.

Under the Venetians, the functions attributed to Butrint as a relatively modest centre were basically two: to stand guard over the Corfu Straits, and utilize the fisheries. The castle housing nowadays the museum was set up to this effect. A castle was built on the other bank of the Vivar Channel for them to exercise direct control over the fisheries. The last domination of Butrint belongs to Ali Pasha, who refortified the Venetian castle located on the shores of the Vivar Channel, as depicted by the French Louis Dupré in a painting of 1819.

In 1928 the Italian archaeologist L. M. Ugolini started the archaeological excavations in Butrint, making sensational discoveries such as the Scaean Gate, the Well of Junia Rufina, the Roman baths, the baptistery, and above all, the theatre. Excavations in Butrint resumed in the 1970s under the direction of Dh. Budina.

THE MONUMENTS OF THE PRASAEBEAN PERIOD
Archaic and Classical City Wall

The acropolis represents the first nucleus of the ancient city, where a mid-7th-century BC fortification occupying an area of 0.7 hectares is still standing. To a second period belong a mid-5th century wall, constructed out of rough-hewn large limestone blocks and a 2.30 m wide entrance walled up by mediaeval constructions.

The real city, enclosed by a 700 metre long wall of large polygonal and trapezoidal blocks, was laid out on its foundations by the early 4th century BC. Throughout its existence as a city the area located on the north-facing hill slope has basically been the most highly populated area of Buthrotum. In ancient times a dividing wall (*diateichisma*) to the south separated this area from the *agora*.

The best preserved part of the Buthrotum circuit-wall runs around the lake shores, with three out of its six main gates, being constructed on this side. The wall constructed out of limestone blocks fitted together without mortar was primarily laid out there towards the turn to the 4th century BC. Its best conserved section built of large trapezoidal blocks is found adjacent to the **Scaean Gate**. Ugolini conventionally borrowed the name for this gate from Virgil's description of Aeneas's entrance to Buthrotum. The 8.50 m long passageway has survived intact with its tone architraves placed across the doorway at the height of 5 m. It was also Ugolini who named the **gate of Lion** after the archaic relief, depicting a lion devouring a bull's head, which was reused for the rebuilding of the gate at a later period.

Remains of the ancient city wall, into which a two-towered gate was inserted in the latter part of the 3rd century BC, can be seen in front

Aerial view of Buthrotum.

The Ksamil peninsula, between the Lake Butrint and the straits of Corfu.

The Lake Butrint, main source of the ancient life in Buthrotum.

Buthrotum and the Vrina plain, the ancient area of the Prasaibes.

The Vivari Channel and the straits of Corfu from the acropolis of Buthrotum.

View of the Scaean Gate.

Nike in front of tropaion. Attic relief of the end of the 5th century BC.

of the gateway to the basilica. The outer gateway to the agora, 2.80 m wide, is found opposite the Sanctuary of Asclepius. In the 3rd century BC a frontage courtyard with a vaulted gateway was laid out to enhance its security.

The Agora

The main political, social and religious activities in the Prasaebean Koinon took place in Buthrotum's agora. The Sanctuary of Asclepius and a *stoa* for the pilgrims were built there by the late 4th century BC. The establishment of the theatre and the *prytaneion* dates back to the mid-3rd century BC.

The Theatre

The *cavea* of theatre lies within a square structure, supported by lateral walls reinforced with buttresses, in imitation of a well-known model of the theatre at Dodona. The stairway has five divisions, with six shallow steps each. The seats in the first row of seating assigned for the dignitaries, the *proedria*, carry special lion-leg relief. In the Roman times, a few holes cut into several blocks served for tying the tents. Being calculated to take the inhabitants of the city and the koinon, the theatre would have given a capacity of about 2500 people.

Entrance to the theatre was via the lateral passageways, where 29 acts relating to the freeing of slaves, dating to 230-167 BC, have been exposed.

Under the Romans two more galleries (*vomitoria*) were added to the staircase at either side for convenience of access to the spectators, who could reach their seats arranged in a Roman-style layout. Also the stage was laid out on a foundation of blocks rising as a wall with three arcades and six niches inserted into it. Its front

The Scaean Gate. Built about 380 BC.

The Lion Gate. Built about 380 and reconstructed about 230 BC.

*The Tower Gate.
About 230 BC.*

*Ideal reconstruction of the
Tower Gate (by G. Pani).*

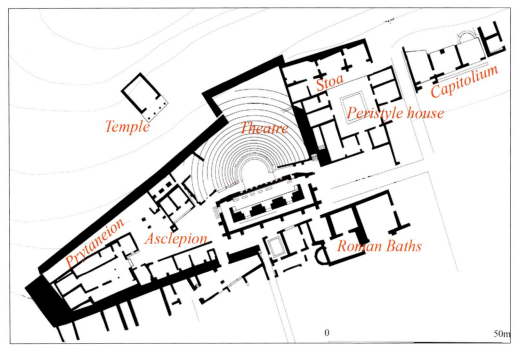
Buthrotum. Plan of the ancient agora.

A legend associate the city with the miracle of Saint Terinus, a local Christian condemned to being fed to the wild beasts in the city theatre.

SANCTUARY OF ASCLEPIUS

The Sanctuary of Asclepius, on the left-hand side of the theatre, was erected over an early prostyle temple, having a *pronaos* and a *naos*. A small window at the northern corner of the naos opened onto the sacred spring. An inscription dedicated by the priest of Asclepius indicated that the temple was devoted to the god of health.

At the turn of the 2nd century AD the temple was reconstructed in the shape of a rectangular building measuring 8.80 x 6.15 m, and was covered with a massive vault. The body of a woman's statue was uncovered by Ugolini on the frontage to the Sanctuary of Asclepius, whereas the head was unearthed in the neighborhood in the course of excavations conducted by Dh. Budina. The archaisant treatment of the coiffure finds parallels in the portrait of Livia, wife of Emperor Augustus. Another small temple was erected somewhere around the mid-3rd century BC, on the natural terrace above the Sanctuary of Asclepius. The location adjacent to the theatre might imply its association with Dionysius.

was formerly covered in multicolored marble, and adorned with sculptures.

The best known is the so-called *Dea* of Butrint. The head placed on a female body statue and the female look in the face was sufficient reason for Ugolini to initially describe it as a local goddess (*Dea di Butrinto*). Later on, he separated the head from the statue, and identified the former as the Praxitelean-type Apollo. The high-quality execution of the sculpture could account for it being a gift presented by the important Roman families, settled in Buthrotum during the Flavian dynasty (69-96 AD).

An other sculpture, dating way back to the latter quarter of the 1st century BC, depicts the Roman strategus Agrippa, with robust features and a concentrated expression of will-power, who, as a Roman author puts it, "…obeyed to one person only (Augustus), but ordered all the rest."

The Buthrotum theatre remained in use until Christendom was officially introduced at the turn of the 4th century AD.

PRYTANION

In the mid-3rd century BC, the square west of the Sanctuary of Asclepius was flanked by the *prytaneion,* built out of rectangular blocks. The centre of the building was occupied by. The peristyle of Ionic order around a rectangular courtyard was the only one space in the building and served as the headquarters of the koinon's strategus. A large Latin inscription in bronze letters, formerly carved in the slabs lying in front

The agora of Buthrotum from the acropolis.

Buthrotum. Aerial view of agora.

Early morning in the agora of Buthrotum.

The theatre of Buthrotum. Middle of the 3rd century BC.

Ideal reconstruction of the Roman stage (by P. Ceschi).

"Dea of Butrinto" in front of theatre of Buthrotum after the discovering by L. M. Ugolini.

Excavations directed by L.M. Ugolini in the theatre of Buthrotum during 1928.

Apollo. Roman copy from a Greek model of the first half of the 4th century BC, considered by Ugolini as "Dea di Butrinto".

Statue of a goddess, or muse. Roman copy of the 1st century AD from a Greek model of first half of the 4th century BC. Lost during Second World War.

ARCHAEOLOGICAL TREASURES FROM ALBANIA 165

The head of Apollo. Roman copy from a Greek model of first half of the 4th century BC, considered by Ugolini as "Dea di Butrinto".

Slave freedom (manumission) decrees on the western parodos of the theatre. About 230- 167 BC.

Asclepius - Aesculapius. Marble relief of the 2nd century AD found in his sanctuary.

The altar of Dionysus in the orcestra of the theatre, with the representation of theatrical masks. 2nd century AD.

The sanctuary of Asclepius- Aesculapius. 2nd century AD.

View toward the prytaneion from the Asclepion.

The turtles, permanent inhabitants of the Asclepion.

Latin inscription dedicated to Germanicus by Caius Iulius Strabo, duumvir quinquenalis of the colony. Between 12-13 AD.

Marble portrait of Augustus from a statue dedicated to him by the Roman colonists of Buthrotum.

Marble portrait of Livia, wife of Augustus, found in Buthrotum. Begin of the 1st century AD.

Buthrotum. Portrait of Marcus Vipsianus Agrippa, who visited Buthrotum in 31 BC, during his campaign against Marc Antony and Cleopatra. 1st century BC.

Another portrait of M. V. Agrippa found in Buthrotum. 1st century BC.

The stoa of the 3rd century BC and the well of the 1st century AD.

THE MONUMENTS OF ROMAN PERIOD

In the Roman period, the city underwent further expansion, incorporating the whole area separating the agora from the Channel. The space of agora was gradually transformed: the main square was paved with stone slabs, the prytaneion was restored as an office for the colonial administration and a new temple, the capitolium, was constructed. During the reign of Augustus a new city quarter together with its forum grew up around the area beyond the Channel, in the actual Vrina plain, and an aqueduct was constructed to furnish it with water. In the Hadrian's period (117-138 AD), when the aqueduct crossed the channel through a bridge, bringing fresh water to the city, the forum came back in the old space of agora. The reconstruction of the stage of theatre and the temple of Asclepius belongs to this period, also the construction of baths, *nymphaeum* and other monuments.

of the building, is associated with the name of Cn.Domitius Eros, who contributed financially to the reconstruction of the prytaneion, and the flooring of the square during 16-12 BC. The construction of a small nymphaeum could also be ascribed to the same period.

STOA

Another building from the Hellenistic period complex survives at the foothill, to the east of the theatre. The monument, 30.50 m long, consisted of one single room that was accessed from four gateways, covered by false arches. No great pains were taken to decorate its interior, given its function as a stoa for pilgrims, visiting the Sanctuary of Asclepius.

A monumental well nearby the stoa belongs to the same complex. The deep-going traces incised by the ropes on the well-head *orthostat*, demonstrate that it continued in use for a long time up until Late Antiquity.

ROMAN BATHS

They have been discovered four Roman baths in Buthrotum. The biggest one, situated in the center of the city, south of the theatre, was partially excavated by Ugolini. The *caldarium* (sized 9.70 x 6.70 m), is better preserved with its floor supported by brickwork pillars (*hypocaust*), which provided the necessary space for the distribution of heat. Three gateways connected the caldarium with the other rooms. The *tepidarium* served as a room for people to adapt themselves to the changes in temperature seated on marble benches backing against the walls. Another hall, covered in white and black mosaic, served as frigidarium. The *opus incertum* employed in the central hall is a typical construction technique during the reign of Emperor Hadrian (117-138 AD).

A big Roman bath measuring 20.15 x 18.33 m lies underneath the great basilica. An *apodyterium* and a *tepidarium*, both covered with mosaics, are partially excavated. Another bath, excavated near the channel, has the main rooms organized around a central domed

Dwelling with a peristyle court near the theatre. 2nd century AD.

Capitolium: the sanctuary of Jupiter, Juno and Minerva, built after the installation of a Roman colony in Buthrotum. About 30 BC.

The Roman baths near the theatre. 2nd century AD.

tepidarium, measuring 15 x 13 m. The baths were 2nd century AD and remained in use in the 3rd century.

Capitolium

In the first decades of the Roman colony a sanctuary was constructed to the central part of the main square. It has three rooms preceded by a portico and e high monumental staircase, typical for the Roman temples of the Augustan period. A Latin inscription dedicated to Minerva, and the specific typology of the building suggest its function as a *capitolium*, consecrated to the main gods of Romans: Jupiter, Junona and Minerva.

Dwellings with Atrium

To the east of the theatre a large building with *atrium* was excavated. It has a 12.50 x 13.50 m sized square courtyard enclosed by a peristyle of 12 Ionic colonnes, comprises the heart of the building. Despite the monumental appearance of the building, its interior is simple, and excavations have not produced any works of art. Its incorporation into the theatre and the Asclepion complex could attribute to it the quality of a public hotel for the guests or actors during feasts to it. The construction technique is a reference point suggesting a 2nd-century AD date for the earliest phase of this building, being in use until the 4th century.

Gymnasium

A monumental building, styled by archaeologists as a gymnasium, is found on the left-hand side on the way from the theatre to the baptistery. Its central part was occupied by a *palaestra* measuring 25 x 12.30 m. The eastern half of the room was dressed with mosaic consisting of bands filled with various motifs, of which that of a wild boar survives. A small, rectangular *nymphaeum* is standing in the centre of the room.

In the niches into the northeastern wall of the monument, the Dionysius's face and two canthars carrying wine branches as his symbol can be seen. The gymnasium represents a public building erected in the 2nd century AD, when the Roman forum, constructed on the site of a pre-existing agora, was left outside the city's former wall.

Nymphaeum

A monumental fountain, in the shape of a rectangular structure, rises on the left-hand side on the way to the great basilica. A wide basin supplied with water from the outlets in the three niches is located beyond its 7 m long façade, all dressed originally with white marble slabs. The water running through the outlets was drawn directly from the city aqueduct of which piers are still visible at either side of the monument. The nymphaeum is a typical Roman construction in *opus testaceum*.

Excavations of the nymphaeum have brought to light a statue of young Dionysius.

Well of Junia Rufina

On the left-hand side of the entrance to the Lion Gate a flight of stone steps runs down to a monumental well nestled at the foot of a natural rock-face. The dedicatory Greek inscription carved in the slab reads: "Junia Rufina, friend of nymphs". Hence, besides having a practical function, the well was also associated with the cult of nymphs as protectors of water springs.

The cult of nymphs, escorts of Pan, is also confirmed by a legend recounted by Plutarch. According to him, Thamos, the pilot of a ship passing the island of Paxos, south of Corcyra, heard from land a voice ordering him to shout the news of Pan's death over the Pelodes Lake (Lake Butrint). "When the ship approached the Pelodes Lake," Plutarch records, "Thamos turned towards land, and shouted out that Great Pan had died. No sooner had he called out the news than he was immediately answered by hundreds of forlorn cries from many creatures yelling together."

Marble statue of Agrippina Junior, mother of Nero. First half of the 1st century AD.

BYZANTINE MONUMENTS

Buthrotum was located in a highly seismic area, and as a result of the tectonic deformations the lower part of the city overflowed with water. Initially perceived as early as the first centuries of the Christian era; during the 5th-6th centuries AD this phenomenon turned into a terrible affliction for the city, which was driven to move to higher locations, thus abandoning the old *agora* area. During this time, the city was fortified with a new circuit-wall, partly rising on the ancient wall foundations, and partly stretching along the Channel bank to the southeast.

The uppermost part of the city was refortified in the mediaeval times, mainly during the reign of the Despotate of Epirus and under Venetian rule, leaving out the whole of its lower area facing southwards and southeast.

ARCHIVESCOVAL PALACE

The construction of a *domus,* the palace with a row of rooms laid out around a south-facing courtyard, close by the Channel, dates from the latter part of the 5th century AD, when Buthrotum was converted into an archivescoval centre. The size of and the lack of decoration in the palace could be accounted for by its function as an archivescoval palace. A room laid with a multicoloured mosaic pavement containing geometric designs, found in front of an exedra where a couch could be inserted, should have been designated as a reception area.

The triconch, or the banqueting room for the guests of the palace owner, is located to the east of the central courtyard. It contained three exedras for the insertion of three beds (*triclinia*) on which to recline at meals.

BAPTISTERY

The baptistery is the most important palaeochristian monument. The room for baptism, with 16 granite columns, arrayed in two concentric

The gymnasium of Buthrotum. 2nd - 3rd centuries AD.

The cantharus as the symbol of Dionysus in the wall mosaic of the niches of the nymphaeum.

Marble portrait of Antinoous, lover of the emperor Hadrian. First half of the 2nd century AD.

The nymphaeum: a monumental well of the first half of the 2nd century AD.

Aerial view of the "Bishop's palace" (triconch).

Archaeological excavations in the "Bishop's palace".

Mosaic pavement in one of the rooms of the palace.

The baptistery.

Aerial view of the baptistery.

Eucharist scene in front of the entry to the baptistery.

View on the baptistery with open mosaics.

Details from the mosaics of the baptistery. Second quarter of the 6th century AD.

rows, has a diameter of 13.50 m. The baptismal font, in the middle of the room, has a cross like shape and is dressed with fine marble slabs. The prodigious values of the monument were highlighted by the mosaic pavement consisting of seven circling bands filled with various motifs.

All the designs shown in the mosaic are rich in symbolism of the Christian doctrine. The scene of eucharistia with two peacocks, and the birds pecking at the grapes shot forth from the cantharis symbolize the paradise and the eternal human souls. The font is flanked by two stags drinking from the paradise stream beneath a cross symbolizing the act of baptism.

This mosaic was created towards the first half of 6th century AD and the baptistery ceased to be in use after the 6th century.

Palaeochristian Basilica

This monument was built as a basilical church towards the mid 6th century AD. Surviving in its best of shape over a very long period of time, it continued in use up until the 18th century, with several repairs being made basically to its uppermost part.

The basilica is a simple architectonic construction both internally and externally. The interior of the church measuring 20.15 x 18.33 m was divided into three naves, separated by brickwork arcades and crossed by a *transept* with a semicircular *apse*.

The central nave, 7.30 m high, had two rows of windows to let allow light through for the whole of the interior. The floor was covered with limestone slabs, whereas the transept pavement retains sections of mosaic ascribed to an earlier construction period. The apse with five external faces was typical of the constructions under emperor Justinian (527-565). The mid 10th century and the 13th century, when the area was controlled by the Despotate of Epirus, saw a major rebuilding of the basilica.

MEDIEVAL FORTIFICATIONS

The Venetian tower, called the Fort of Ali Pasha survives intact. A decorative course, typical of the 15th century Venetian constructions, marks the beginning of the first floor that is approached by a staircase. The only one room, measuring 6 x 6 m, is covered with a conic vault. The primary role for the tower - a, as well as the Vivar castle on the other bank of the Channel, was to keep a close watch on the fisheries.

The triangular fortress, to the south of the Vivar channel, opposite Buthrotum, dates back to the period of Angevin domination (1272-1286). It had the shape of an isosceles triangle measuring 40.50 and 51 m along the sides. A chain of slits positioned along a pathway running around the walls and two narrow entrances completed the poor architecture of this fortification. Under Venetian domination and the short-lived Turkish rule in the 17th century, the castle was refortified with three towers whose walls were punctuated with cannon ports. During this period a small fishermen's centre grew up around the castle, which survived until the 19th century as shown by an engraving of that time.

The small castle at the mouth of the Vivari channel was constructed in 18th century, but often attributed to Ali Pasha, who, during his short reign in the region, used it to control the ships sailing to Butrint, and thwart sudden French attacks from the sea. The fort is rectangular and the towers had canon ports.

An ancient relief was accidentally found ashore not far from the castle. It shows Nike, in front of a *tropaion* - the symbol of victory, consisting of an enemy breast-plate deposed on a rock. The style, the type of marble and the high quality of its processing confirm the Attic origin of the relief dating to the latter part of the 5th century BC.

Aerial view of the Great Basilica of Buthrotum. On the right side: the nymphaeum and the Tower gate.

The colonnades of the Great Basilica.

View of the Great Basilica. Built in the first half of the 6th century AD and reconstructed in the 13th century.

Tower on the surrounding wall of the 6th century AD.

Venetian Tower near the Vivari Channel, called the "Tower of Ali Pasha". In the foreground, the Roman Baths.

The Triangle Castle of Vivari. Constructed by Venetians and reconstructed during the Turkish occupation.

Ali Pasha with his guards on Butrint Lake, after Louis Dupré (1819).

ANCIENT CENTRES AROUND BUTHROTUM

Çuka e Ajtoit, perhaps the Prasaebean Pergam, was established as a genuine city at the turn of the 4th century BC. The 1.400 m long walls enclosed a densely populated area of 5 hectares. The foundations of a large number of the dwellings were partly cut into the natural rock-face and a palace encircled by terracing walls is discovered to the west, outside the city.

The **Malathrea fortification**, measuring 18 x 18 m and reinforced with rectangular towers on the four corners, is located on the way between Çuka e Ajtoit and Buthrotum. This square fortification was an fortified dwelling, property of one of Epirote landlords living in the 3rd century BC, who are recorded by Polybius, as well.

To the north, the Prasaebes territory was protected by the **Dema Wall**, intersecting the passageway running across the peninsula at the point where the latter juts out in between the lake and the sea. The wall is constructed out of large rectangular stone blocks and falls away towards the sea-shore. The fortification is 5th century BC.

The **Monastery of Saint George** was erected on top of Dema wall in the 19th century. A small church, with its dome overlying the octagonal cylinder and its narthex ending up in a two-windowed bell-tower, are found within the enclosure.

Another ancient fortification is found on the **Kalivo** hill, facing southeast of the lake, across Butrint. A 1.300 m long, very primitive wall defended the hillside looking out onto the plain, while leaving the lakeside approach itself undefended. Three front gateways are inserted on the east side of the wall. The wall is constructed of semi-hewn polygonal blocks. The space within the walls is empty, and the 6th century BC fortification seems to have been built with a view to providing support to the Buthrotum archaic acropolis, and shelter to the rural population. This fortification and the Dema Wall are assigned to a period when Buthrotum was under Corcyra.

Diaporit, where recent excavations have established the presence of a 2nd-3rd century AD luxurious villa, lies along the shores of the lake, to the north of Kalivo. A *hypocaust* provided heating to its numerous rooms of marble-clad floors and painted walls, surrounded by decorative terraces. In the 5th century AD the villa was abandoned, and its walls were brought down so that the material could be used for the construction of a basilica.

The piers of a Roman aqueduct built under Augustus are preserved in the vicinity of the **Xara** village. A main water depot and a separate water-supply for the suburb just beyond the Channel can be seen on the way approaching the Vivar Channel. The aqueduct crossed the Channel over a bridge during the reign of Hadrian (117-135 AD).

Views of the Roman Villa in Diaporit, near Butrint. 2nd century AD.

View of the hill of Kalivo from Butrint.

Part of the façade of the archaic wall of Kalivo. 6th century BC.

The drunken Pan. Bronze figurine found near Butrint. 3rd century BC.

View of the hill of Çuka e Ajtojt from the fortified dwelling of Malathrea. 3rd century BC.

The Northern Gate of the ancient city of Çuka e Ajtojt (Pergamon?). About 380 BC.

Marble portrait of King Pyrrhos found in Herculanum. 3rd century BC.

ANTIGONEIA AND THE ANCIENT CENTRES AROUND IT

The valley of the Drinos was one of the most developed regions in the ancient period. Three important cities and five castles watched over the important natural road that cut through the valley connecting the Illyrian coastal plain with Chaonia and Molossia.

With such a strategic position, the valley could hardly be spared from important events during antiquity. Ancient authors called it Atintania, the southernmost region of Illyria. The ancient Greek historian Thucydides (II, 80, 6) tells us that in 429 BC, the Antintanes were part of the Molossian Kingdom. Around 380 BC the Greek geographer, Pseudo-Scylax, mentions them among the Illyrian peoples who lived "...above Oricum and Chaonia, all the way to Dodona." The centre of the region in this period was a city located on the hill of Melani, the ancient name of which remains unknown.

At the beginning of the 3rd century BC, the valley of the Drinos fell under the rule of Pyrrhus, who founded a new main centre there with the name of Antigoneia. In 230 BC, the Illyrian fleet of Queen Teuta disembarked several thousand warriors by surprise in the harbour of Onchesmos (Saranda), who had previously conquered Phoenice, the

The gorges of the river Vjosa near Tepelena, known as "Aoos Stenae" during antiquity.

The view of the hill of Jerma, where the ancient city of Antigoneia was situated.

capital of Epirus. Another Illyrian army of 5,000 warriors had passed through the narrow mountain passages near Antigoneia and attacked in stealth the Epirotes and their allies who had come to the aid of Phoenice. Polybius (II, 5, 8) tells us that "...the Epirotes were defeated, many were killed and many taken prisoner; the others escaped and went to the Antintanes." There is no doubt that those Atintanes were residents of the upper valley of the Drinos, around Antigoneia.

In 229 BC, the Roman senate sent a fleet of 200 ships against the Illyrians, which, after taking control of Corfu, sailed in the direction of Apollonia, where it met up with the Roman infantry, which had disembarked there from Brundisium, under the leadership of the other consul, L. Postumus. After they took Dyrrhachium and subjected the Ardianes, and according to Polybius (II, 11, 11) "...they were joined by the Parthines and Atintanes, who sent envoys to subject themselves

voluntarily...". This surely means the area behind Apollonia, where the *koinon* of the Atintanes extended, along the central valley of the river Aoos and the valley of the Drinos, as well as the area behind Dyrrhachium, where the *koinon* of the Parthines was located.

From the time of these events, the Atintanes took on a strategic importance for the Roman senate. They inhabited an area from which the roads leading from Apollonia to Epirus and Macedonia could be controlled, and also from which those two states could be isolated from a possible alliance against Rome.

Philip V of Macedonia conquered Atintania in 211 BC and used it as a base for attacking Apollonia. In 198 BC, Philip V decided to undertake a military campaign against Epirus and appeared with his army at the narrows of the Aoos, near the modern village of Dragot in the Tepelena district. But Rome did not just stand by; a Roman army

The acropolis and the basileia of Antigoneia.

under the leadership of consul Titus Flaminius sailed from Corfu to Chaonia, went through Atintania and appeared at the narrows of the Aoos, where it broke the army of Philip V, which withdrew hastily for Macedonia through the valley of the Aoos.

In 169 BC, when King Gentius of the Illyrians, who ruled from Lissus in the north, and King Perseus of Macedonia started military action against the Romans, the residents of Antigoneia took the side of the Romans. In a battle against the Macedonians that took place in a field before their city, the Antigoneians suffered a crushing defeat. Livy, who describes this event, does not tell us what brought victory to the Macedonians. One possibility is that they attacked and burned the city of Antigoneia. That would fit with the traces of fire that have been found during archaeological excavations in many residences of the city, as well as with the fact that from that time, Antigoneia is abandoned as a city. It is also possible that Antigoneia was included in the list of 170 Epirote cities that were destroyed in 167 BC by consul Aemilius Paullus. The ancient historians are silent after this event, and the memory of the city built by Pyrrhus remains only in geographical maps and notations.

It would be the archaeologist Dhimosten Budina, who in 1966 began archaeological excavations on the hill of Jerma and would revive the name of Antigoneia once more. In 1969, he found 14 round tablets of bronze, with a diameter of only 2 cm but which were stamped with the name of the *koinon* of the citizens of Antigoneia.

ANTIGONEIA

The ancient city of Antigoneia extends over the hill of Jerma, to the southwest of the village of Saraqinisht in the Lunxhëria region. It was founded about 295 BC by Pyrrhus of Epirus, to immortalise the name of his wife, Antigone.

FORTIFICATIONS OF THE CITY

With a circumference of 3700 m, the surrounding wall of Antigoneia is third after that of Apollonia and Phoenice. The highest part of the fortification, the *acropolis,* has an area of 3 ha and is divided from the residential area by a wall reinforced with seven rectangular towers. The entire other part of the fortification is surrounded with a single

Poseidon. Bronze figurine found in Antigoneia. 3rd century BC.

Postern in the southern surrounding wall of Antigoneia. About 290 BC.

Bucolic scene on the surrounding wall.

Aerial view of the centre of the ancient city.

Plan of the ancient city of Antigoneia.

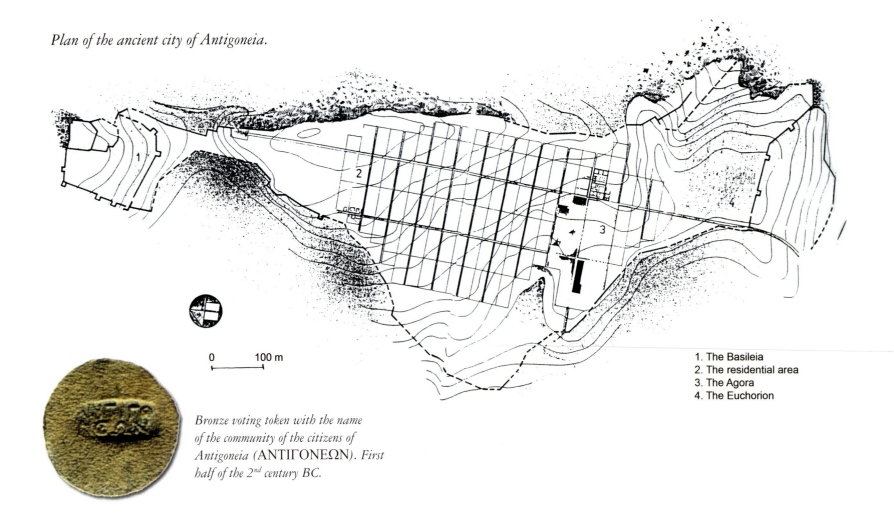

1. The Basileia
2. The residential area
3. The Agora
4. The Euchorion

Bronze voting token with the name of the community of the citizens of Antigoneia (ΑΝΤΙΓΟΝΕΩΝ). First half of the 2nd century BC.

wall, reinforced with towers in the places most exposed to possible enemy attacks. The whole southern wing of the fortification was similar, with towers placed so that enemy forces would come between two fires during an attack. One of the main entrances to the city, the one that was the principal axis cutting through the city from north to south, could also be defended from those towers. The road corridor passed between two towers, in a manner similar to that of the southern gate of the city of Lissus (Lezha). Another entrance, only 1 metre wide, was located almost in the middle of the southern wall and served for warriors to make a dramatic exit during counterattacks. The surrounding wall of Antigoneia was constructed of conglomerate limestone blocks in rectangular forms, set in parallel lines of equal height (*isodomic*). It was characteristic that it was kept at the same height, which was related to the fact that the wall of limestone blocks served as the base on which an adobe structure up to 7 m high was built. This manner of construction is known from the surrounding wall of Apollonia in the 4th – 3rd centuries BC, as well as in the surrounding wall of the *agora* of Butrint.

The construction of the fortifications of Antigoneia was accompanied by the erection of other fortifications in the valley of the Drinos, which formed a single system of protection for upper Atintania. They show the same construction technique used in the fortifications of Lekli, Melani, Ktismata and others. A more distant influence is found in Lissus, where a similar plan was applied.

The street of the agora with the foundations of the stoa. Middle of the 3rd century BC

Parts of a bronze equestrian statue, found in the stoa of Antigoneia. First half of the 3rd century BC.

Bronze instrument for the castration of bulls, found in Antigoneia. First half of the 2nd century BC.

Doric colonnade in the portico of the prytaneion. 3rd century BC.

The agora

The city was constructed in a short time and according to a single plan. One surrounding wall 3700 m in length enclosed the hill's high plain, including four areas with different functions. On the highest part, a transverse wall *basileia* stood out; this was the place where Pyrrhus and Antigone lived when they were able to come to the city. The *agora* was placed in the central part. The flat areas by the main entrance to the city in the south were reserved for the *euchorion*. It was here that residents of the city's surroundings were sheltered during time of war, together with any property they might have been able to take with them.

The remaining surface was designated for residences, according to the Hippodamic system. A network of roads laid at right angles divided up the area that was to be inhabited into *insula* 106 m long and 53 m wide, with an approximately equal number of residences. The principal roads, 7 m wide, formed north-south axes. The two main roads crossed at the entrance to the *agora*, which extended over an area equal to six *insula* (about 3 hectare or ha).

Of the public monuments of the city, only the *stoa* and the *prytaneion* have been discovered.

Main street starting from the centre of Antigoneia.

The *stoa* was found on the highest part of the *agora* and is bounded on the south by the main road. A construction 59 m long and 9,50 m wide, it was divided lengthwise by the colonnade, creating two paths for walking. An extension of the construction on the west wing permitted the installation of an enclosed circular staircase leading to the second storey. The entire southern facade of the monument was open, making it possible for the public to pass through the colonnades toward the main square of the *agora*. Similar monuments, both in form and dimensions, which served as public strolling areas, have been found in Cassopea of Thesprotia and in Byllis.

During the excavation of the *stoa*, parts of a group sculptured in bronze were found. The tail of a horse, a special helmet for horses and a piece of a sword belong to the statue of a man on horseback, while a delicate feminine hand with a ring on her finger shows that there was also a statue of a woman. It can be thought that they remained after the destruction of a sculptural group presenting Pyrrhus on a horse and his wife, Antigone, beside him.

The Prytaneion. The *prytaneion* was found at the intersection of the main roads that separate the *agora* from the residential area. It has a rectangular plan with dimensions of 18 x 8,20 m. The monument's

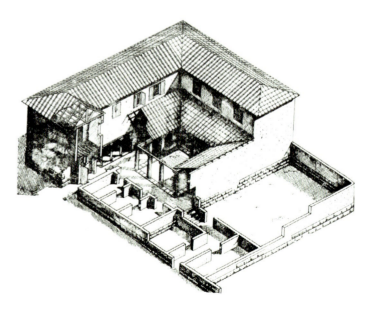

Dwelling with peristyle court and its ideal reconstruction. 3rd century BC.

facade was decorated with a colonnade of four Doric columns. Behind the narrow vestibule, there was a connection to the monument's two alcoves, according to a model known from *prytaneion* found in Byllis and in Cassopea. In fact, the highest city official in Antigoneia had the function of *strategus*, which was a tradition of the cities of Epirus.

The residences. Archaeological excavations conducted by Dhimosten Budina in Antigoneia during 1966-1990 were principally focussed on uncovering the residences of the ancient city. A **residence with peristyle** discovered to the south of the road of the *agora* belonged to a wealthy citizen. It has a rectangular plan with a total area of

ARCHAEOLOGICAL TREASURES FROM ALBANIA 213

Foot of a large bronze vase in the shape of a sphinx. 3rd century BC.

Human figure from the mosaic of the basilica of Antigoneia. 6th century AD.

660 m². An internal courtyard of rectangular shape represented the centre of the architectonic formulation, surrounded by a *peristyle* of twelve Ionic columns. On its east side, the three principal rooms of the residence were found. The house had a second storey and was built of rectangular stones, over which rose adobe walls.

During the excavation of the residence, a burned layer was found, testimony to the destruction of this residence by fire during the events of 167 BC. After this, attempts were made to re-build part of it, apparently by residents who escaped the catastrophe.

A second part of the residence, developed on the west of the house with a *peristyle,* was called **the artisan's residence** by Budina, because he found work implements and bronze vessels there, related to the handicraft activity of its residents. He also found a large rectangular stone with a number of holes of different sizes, which could have served as a measuring device for the grain for which the artisanal products might have been exchanged.

The house of Pyrrhus was what Budina called the third residence, laid out south of the main road, where the space of the *agora* began, because during its excavation, a round stone vessel was found that bore the inscription "Pyrrhus." Also found there was the foot of a large bronze vessel moulded in the form of a sphinx.

The most interesting discovery was made in the **general's house,** in the north-western part of the city. During the excavation of its rooms, there were found a beautiful bronze figurine of the god Poseidon, a round mud seal with a symbol of a thunderbolt and the inscription ΣΤΡΑΤΑΓΟΥ ("of the general"), as well as 14 pieces of round tokens that bore the inscription ΑΝΤΙΓΟΝΕΙΩΝ ("of the citizens of Antigoneia"). It is thought that they might have served for voting. A number of broken mud vessels, a bronze vessel showing signs of burning, and scattered bronze coins on the floor of the room revive the scene of the raiding and burning of the building by the city's attackers.

Paleo-Christian Church

During the 1974 excavations, Dhimosten Budina discovered an early Christian church in the southeast corner of the city. Its dimensions were 13.80 x 4.60 m and it was in the form of a *triconch*, with three apses closing the altar on the eastern side.

The floor of the altar was laid with a multi-coloured mosaic extending over an elliptical area between two of the apses. The central panel contains the figure of a person with the head of a dog, with his left hand raised high, as if he is going to strike a large snake. Four inscriptions in the mosaic refer to the persons who sponsored or realised it. The human figure has been explained as St. Christopher, who appeared as a man with the head of a dog, while the construction of the church has been dated to the 6th century AD. In this period there was no important residential location in the territory of Antigoneia, while the level of realisation of the mosaic and the inscriptions themselves attest to wealthy and cultured persons. Significant signs of fire on the surface of the mosaic show that the church was destroyed, probably during the Slavic invasions of the 6th century AD.

THE MONASTERY OF ST. MARY IN SPILE

The monastery of St. Mary is located about 2 km to the east of Antigoneia. It was built on a cliff of conglomerate limestone, known as Spile because of the caves (from Greek spile = cave) of karst, one of which was inhabited by Eremites.

The church is in good condition. It consists of a *naos*, of the type in the form of a cross with cupola, narthex and narrow gallery. Over the gate of the naos is an inscription in Greek, saying that the church was painted by Michael in the year 1634. A second inscription, bearing the date of 1659, speaks of the painting of the *pronaos* with icons, with the contribution of the *archon* John.

The frescos are of high quality and can be compared with those of Voskopoja.

The Church of Saint Mary in the Monastery of Spile, 17th century.

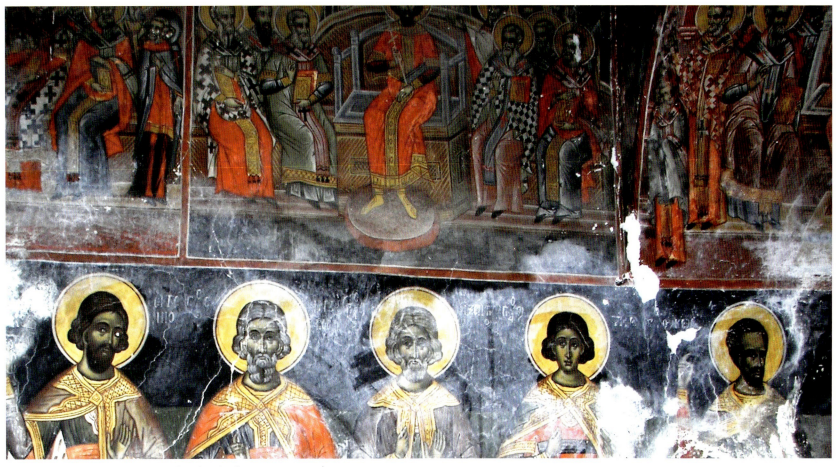
Christ and the prophets. Fresco in the Church of Saint Mary. 17th century.

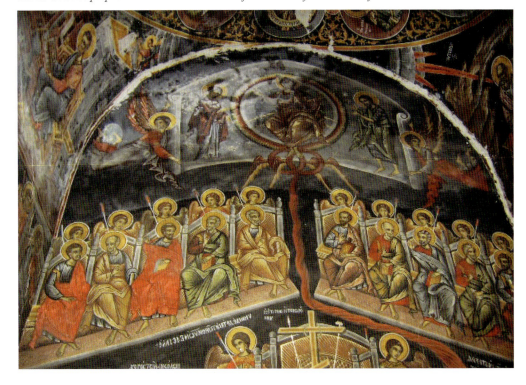
The Saints. Fresco from the Church of Saint Mary. 17th century.

Hermit's cave near the monastery of Spile, near Antigoneia.

House in the village of Saraqinisht, near Antigoneia.

The gate of the house.

Reliefs with figures from popular mythology on the gate of the house.

OTHER ANCIENT SITES IN THE VALLEY OF THE DRINOS

The castle of Greater Labova (Labova e Madhe) is found about 500 m south of the village of the same name. With a surface area of about 1.4 ha, the ancient fortification surrounds the highest part of a cliff, leaving the southern part open, which is protected by nature. A trapezoidal bastion and another semi-circular one controlled the approach to the castle from the side of the mountain pass, where the entrance was located. Over its entire length the wall presents a kind of terrace, up to 5 m high, built with large tiles of stone extracted from the limestone layers. Traces of residences are preserved within the castle, and ceramic fragments, dating from the beginning of habitation in this castle in the 5th century BC, have also been found there.

The ancient city on the slope of Melani. On the range of hills that border the valley of the Drinos on the southeast, the Slope of Melani catches one's eye. It is a rocky platform covered by a cypress forest, separated by a low pass from the side of Bureto Mountain. The upper part of the hill, with an area of about 8 ha, was in antiquity surrounded by a wall about 1100 m long. For its entire length, the wall was built with large limestone blocks, in polygonal forms, and it resembles walls of the same kind in Phoenice, Butrint and Çuka e Ajtojt. On the eastern side, where the traces of three rectangular towers can be made out, the wall changes entirely so far as concerns the building technique. Here it consists of rectangular limestone blocks placed in rows of equal height. This particularity shows that there was a second period of construction, contemporaneous with Antigoneia.

On the flat upper plains of the northern side of the residential area,

View of the hill of Melan, where the ancient centre of the valley of Drinos was situated before the foundation of Antigoneia.

where there are natural springs of drinking water, traces of buildings that served a social function are preserved. On the south side, the foundations of another such building with a rectangular plan can be seen, as well as the traces of a mosaic from Roman times.

The ancient city on the Slope of Melani was constructed in the first half of the 4th century BC as the major urban centre for the region. After Antigoneia was built, it remained in the role of a castle, as shown by the partial reconstruction of the surrounding wall. During the reign of Justinian (527 – 565 AD), parts of the western and southern walls of the city were rebuilt. In an even later period, about the 12th to the 14th century, there was another reconstruction of the wall, as well as an irrigation system in the form of a wall through which a ceramic tube passed.

Later buildings on the Slope of Melani are represented by a Bektashi tekke.

Hadrianopolis. In the middle of the valley of the Dropull, facing the Slope of Melani, the ancient city of Hadrianopolis has been found. It was founded during the reign of the Emperor Hadrian (117 – 138 AD) and is shown in the Peutingerian Map (Tabula Peutingeriana) as the third way station on the road from Apollonia to Nicopolis. Geophysical research has shown that it extended over an area of about 16 ha and was traversed by a quadratic network of roads. Archaeological excavations, which were begun by Apollon Baçe, have brought to light the city's ancient theatre, in a central area that must have been the forum.

The theatre is of the well-known Roman type, built on flat terrain with the seating area supported by a semicircular wall of a diameter of 57.23 m and a height that reached 15 m. There were 24 rows of seats in all, made of limestone blocks, seating about 3500 – 4000 spectators. The stage consisted of a low rostrum (*pulpitum*), behind which rose the stage wall (*frons scenae*), treated with a simple wall construction of engraved stones. The entrance to the theatre was from

Part of the surrounding wall of Melan. Beginning of the 4th century BC.

two doors in the front at each side of the stage as well as through two stone stairways in the perimeter wall, for the upper rows of the seating area. The entire monument was oriented to the northeast, where the forum was found.

Archaeological excavations tell us that the theatre was destroyed during the 4th to 6th centuries AD, when materials ripped out of it were used for other buildings in the square of the forum. It was just at that time that Hadrionapolis is mentioned by Procopius of Caesarea (De aed.,IV, 1, 36) as a city rebuilt by the Emperor Justinian, who also changed its name to Justinianopolis.

Paleokastra. The castle of Paleokastra is found at the place where the Drinos river meets the Kardhiqi, in front of the mountain declivity where Antigoneia is located. Archaeological excavations have determined that the castle extended in the form of a regular trapezoid with an area of almost 1 ha, sufficient for a cohort of a Roman legion (1000 soldiers). The surrounding walls are reinforced by 16 towers and had four entrances on the castle's main axes, according to criteria of a Roman military camp. Excavations along the surrounding walls,

The theatre of the Roman city Hadrianopolis. First half of the 2nd century AD.

The stage of the theatre of Hadrianopolis.

The supporting wall of the theatre.

Excavations in the forum of the city of Hadrianopolis.

on the inside, have uncovered a row of barracks for housing soldiers. On the east side of the castle, an early Christian basilica, from the 5th century AD, was excavated. It was built simply, the only embellishments being architectonic fragments of white marble that belonged to the iconostasis.

Another early Christian church was discovered about 100 m outside of the castle walls and was linked to the city's necropolis.

A Latin inscription found during excavations in the castle dates its construction to the period of the joint rule of the Emperors Constantine and Licinius, in the years 311-324 AD.

ARCHAEOLOGICAL TREASURES FROM ALBANIA 225

*The surrounding wall of the castle of Paleokastra.
First quarter of the 4th century AD.*

*Ideal reconstruction of the main gate
of the castle of Paleokastra.*

The medieval Castle of Gjirokastra, which replaced Antigoneia as the main center of Drinos Valley.

The gorges of River Vjosa near Tepelena, known as "Aous Stenae", where the battle between the Roman Army of Flaminius and Macedonians of King Philipp V was fought in 198 BC.

*The ancient and medieval Castle of Këlcyra
on the eastern side of the gorges of River Vjosa near Përmeti.*

GLOSSARY

Acropolis	The upper fortified part of an ancient city.
Agonothetus	A public official charged with the responsibility for organising public games, sporting events, feasts, etc.
Agora	Market of a city; later, the public square.
Amphora	A Greek or Roman two-handled vessel, as a container for wine, or oil.
Analemma	Wall supporting the stairway of a theatre.
Andron	Room of the master of the house, where guests and friends were received.
Atrium	Inner courtyard surrounded with a portico.
Apse	A large semicircular or polygonal recess, arched or dome-roofed, at the end of a church).
Aqueduct	A conduit or artificial channel for conveying water, supported by arches.
Arrybal	Greek oil jag.
Asclepius	The god of healing and medicine: identified with the Roman god Aesculapius.
Asclepion	Sacred precinct round the Sanctuary of Asclepius.
Atrium	Inner courtyard surrounded with a portico.
Attic	Originally from a region dominated by Athens.
Baptistery	A part of the church used for baptismal services.
Basileia	Part of a Hellenistic city where the palace of the King was situated.
Basilica	An oblong building with a broad nave flanked by colonnaded aisles or porticoes ending in a semicircular apse.
Bastion	A fortified outwork, often in quadrangular form, projecting from the main wall in the same high.
Boucranion	Ornamentation in the form of an ox head.
Boulé	City Council.
Caldarium	Hot room in a Roman bath.
Cantharus	A deep cup with two vertical handles above the brim; one of symbols associated with Dionysius.
Capital	The head or cornice of pillar or column.
Cardo maximus	The main street north-south in a Roman castrum.
Castrum	*A Roman military camp in a quadratic plan.*
Cavea	The concave auditorium of a theatre; a theatre.
Colonnade	A series of columns placed at regular intervals and supporting an entablature.
Concha	A vaulted (domed) apse.
Conistra	A deep orchestra adapted for the gladiators contests in an ancient theatre.
Cornucopia	Goat's horn depicted as a horn of plenty, overflowing with flowers, fruit and corn.
Damiurgos	Representative of a region in the koinon.
Damnatio memoriae	Punishment condemning a person by removing his name and appearance.
Damosia	The political urban community or its property.
Decurions	The council of ten men at the head of a Roman colony.
Diaconicon	A part of the church in which religious services were prepared.

Diazoma	A passage in the auditorium of an ancient Greek theatre dividing the lower from the upper rows of seats for convenience of access.
Duumviri	The two principal officials of a colony elected for five years (*quinquenalis*).
Ecclesia	General meeting of free citizens.
Emplekton	Wall with two partitions and the fill between them.
Entablature	The part of a classical building supported by the columns, comprising architrave, frieze, and cornice.
Ephebe	Young man from 18 to 20 years old undergoing military training.
Euchorion	Space within the city walls, designed to house rural inhabitants in case of a war.
Exedra	A semicircular part of a wall in a building.
Exonarthex	Area outside narthex.
Frigidarium	A room in the Roman bath supplied with cold water.
Frieze	In the entablature of an order, the member between the architrave and the cornice.
Frons scenae	Façade of the stage.
Fronton	A pediment.
Grammateus	Secretary.
Gymnasiarchos	Official in charge of the physical training of the youth.
Gymnasium	A public building in which young men received lessons and training.
Hallkoma	Bronze tablet with inscription.
Herm	A squared pillar surmounted by a head or bust. (usu. that of Hermes), used as a boundary-marker, or gravestone.
Hypparchos	A public official - commander of the cavalry.
Hypocaust	A hollow space or flues under floor or within walls, in which heat from furnace was accumulated for heating house or bath.
Impluvium	The square basin in the centre of the atrium of a Roman house, which received rainwater from an opening in the roof.
In situ	An archaeological object, or context found in its original place.
Insula (pl. ~*lae*)	Block of residences between two principal roads in a city (from Latin "island").
Isodomic	Stile of masonry using blocks in rectangular forms, set in parallel lines of equal height.
Koinon	The political union of regions and cities.
Krepis	Base made of blocks of a wall of bricks or adobe.
Naos	Principal room of a church, or temple.
Narthex	A raided-off antechamber or porch at the western end of some churches.
Nave	The main part or body of a temple or church, usu. extending from the west door to the chancel and *freq.* separated from the aisle on each side by pillars.
Necropolis	Cemetery near a city; an ancient burying-place.
Nymphaeum	A water grotto, or a fountain, or shrine dedicated to a nymph or nymphs.
Nymphs	Minor divinities of nature, represented as beautiful maidens dwelling in the mountains, forests, meadows, and waters.
Obelisk	A stone pillar devoted to Apollo.
Opus	In Latin - "work;" used with the following words for types of Roman wall construction:
- *coementicum*	with a mixture of stones and mortar.
- *mixtum*	with a mixture of brick belts and stones.
- *incertum*	with irregular stones in the facade.
- *quadratum*	with rectangular blocks.
- *reticulatum*	with stones or bricks in the form of a mesh.
- *testaceum*	with a dressing of bricks.
- *sectile*	a floor with figures of pieces of marble slabs.
Orchestra	A semicircular space used by the actors and chorus in front of the proscenium in an ancient theatre.

Order	A system or style of building subject to certain uniform established proportions, decoration, (Doric, Ionic, Corinthian, Tuscan and Composite).
Orthogonal	Pertaining to a city planning system with roads in the form of a grid.
Orthostat	An upright stone or slab forming part of a structure or set in the ground.
Palaeochristian	Early Christian period (4th-6th centuries AD).
Parodos	A passage in an ancient Greek theatre between auditorium and scene, by which spectators had access to the theatre.
Patera	A flat metallic dish used in religious ceremonies.
Pax romana	Peace in the Roman Empire in the first and second century AD.
Peripolarchos	A public official- commander of the border guards.
Peripter	Greek temple having a single row of pillars surrounding it.
Peristyle	A row of columns surrounding a building, court, cloister, etc.; the court surrounded by the columns.
Pilaster	A half column or pillar, *esp.* one projecting from a wall.
Politarches	Highest public official of the city.
Praefurnum	The fire place in a Roman bath.
Proedria	The first row of seats in the ancient theatre.
Pronaos	The space in front of the *naos* of a temple, enclosed by a portico and projecting side-walls.
Proscenium	The stage of an ancient theatre.
Prothesis	The part of a church where the credence table stands.
Prytanis	Highest official of the city, elected every year.
Prytaneion	A public building or hall serving as the place of meeting and dining for the public officials.
Pulpitum	A raised platform for actors in a Roman theatre.
Quadriporticus	Open court with porticos on four sides.
Sanctuary	A holy place around a temple or a sacred place; place of the altar in a church (*bema*).
Sima	A stone, decorated eaves on the top of *entablement*.
Spolia	Architectural parts reused in a later.
Stela (pl. ~lae)	An upright slab or pillar, usual bearing a commemorative inscription, or sculptured design and often serving as a gravestone.
Stenae	The narrows or gorge of a river.
Stoa	A portico, walled at the back, with a front colonnade opening on a public place.
Strategus	Elected official, assigned with the defence and leading of the army of the city.
Strigil	A skin-scraper used by bathers or after exercise.
Stylobate	A continuous base supporting row of columns.
Sudatio	The sweat room of public baths.
Synarchontes	Public officials, members of a collegium.
Synthronon	The seat within an apse for the clergy to sit during ceremonies.
Tabula ansata	A flat inscription in a rectangular form with two handles.
Tamias	Official for financial matters.
Temenos	A sacred ground, enclosure, precinct surrounding or adjacent to a temple.
Tepidarium	The room of Roman baths for adapting with the temperature.
Transept	A large space in the front part of a basilica, perpendicular to the naves.
Tribelon	An entrance divided by columns into three.
Triclinium	A couch, running round three sides of a table, on which to recline at meals.
Triconch	A dining-room with apses on the sides for installing triclinia.
Tropaion	A monument consecrated to a victory.

ORIGIN OF ILLUSTRATIONS

Alket Islami: Photos in pages 56 upper, 64 upper, 67, 69 lower, 70, 146, 160, 179, 184 upper, 187, 207.

Apollon Baçe: Photo in page 225.

Archive of the Institute of Archaeology in Tirana: Photos in pages 15, 16, 74 upper, 89 lower.

Butrint Foundation: Photos in pages 145 , 158.

Elio Hobdari: Photos in pages 17, 220.

Engjell Serjani: Photo in page 214.

GIS – ALBANIA: Geographic map of Albania.

Guri Pani: Photo in page 157.

L. M. Ugolini: Photos in pages 96, 100,135,163, 164.

Olgita Ceka: Photos in page 43 upper left and lower, upper middle,

P. Cabanes, M. Korkuti, A. Baçe, N. Ceka, Carte archeologique d'Albanie, Tirana, 2008: Photos in pages 144, 212 lower.

Pullumb Naipi and the author: Photo in page 29 lower.

Schätze aus dem Land der Skipetaren, Mainz, 1988: Photos in pages 1, 10, 31 lower left, 38 lower, 41 right, 51 right and lower, 52 right, 78, 81 left and upper right, 88 lower, 91 right and lower, 93-95, 154, 165, 170 left, 176, 198, 205 right, 208, 209 lower, 213.

Sami Çela and the author: Photos in pages 24 lower, 38 upper.

Skënder Muçaj: Photos in pages 43 upper right, 54 lower, 65 lower right, 66, 68, 221.